UPBRINGING

A Discussion Handbook
For Parents
of Young Children

JAMES B. STENSON

SCEPTER PUBLISHERS

Princeton, New Jersey

Copyright © 1991 by Scepter Publishers, Inc.
All rights reserved.
First printing, 1992
Second printing, 1993

ISBN No. 0-932939-52-9
Printed in the United States of America

Contents

A NOTE TO PARENTS

As YOU CAN TELL from glancing through this handbook, *Upbringing* is a bit unusual.

Unlike most other works on "parenting" and "family-life" issues, this book is not meant to be read silently, all by oneself, from cover to cover. It is, rather, a handbook of selected topics dealing with character-formation in children, and it is meant to be read by couples — husband and wife together, and then groups of couples — as a basis for discussing each of the issues in depth.

Upbringing does not pretend to lay out many clear-cut formulas or recipes for raising children well. It is my firm conviction that there are no such things; there are many different approaches to being a successful parent, as I hope you will see herein. Furthermore, the handbook does not provide a list of concrete suggestions for individual family circumstances. Advice and suggestions generally come forth best, and most effectively, from discussion among experienced parents.

What *Upbringing* does provide is a useful framework for this kind of fruitful discussion. It deals with some simple but important principles in family life and some thought-provoking insights for reflection and then exchange of ideas, all based on people's personal experience.

I have had several reasons for taking this approach. Let me explain them here at the outset.

For more than 20 years, I have worked as a teacher and administrator in two small, excellent schools: The Heights School in Washington, D.C., and Northridge Preparatory School in suburban Chicago. During that time, I befriended a large number of outstanding parents and teachers, people who succeeded exceptionally well in raising children to responsible adulthood. The experiences of these people, together with other

8

studies and interviews I undertook, form the basis for what appears in these pages.

All this experience has convinced me that today's parents have serious needs that are not being met effectively in modern society. *Upbringing* is aimed at addressing those needs, or at least taking some serious steps in that direction.

The first of those needs, acutely felt by conscientious parents, is that of forming a *framework for strategic planning.*

No task is more important than that of dealing effectively with children, leading them to become competent, responsible adults who are committed to living by Christian principles. Like any other great endeavor, this task takes serious planning on a long-term basis, a vision that we may call *strategic thinking.* But the problem is that most parents today are extremely busy with the details of week-to-week family living. It's hard to think long-term, to reflect on the really important questions in family life: Where are we headed? What sort of men and women do we hope our children will grow to be? Are we making progress, and how can we tell? What do we have to do *now* to help our children grow toward responsible adulthood?

Strategic thinking generally deals with the *why,* not the *how,* of action. Experience shows that if *why* questions are asked often enough and deeply enough, the *how* of life generally suggests itself. This kind of thinking calls for forming a few simple principles for action, a framework for evaluating and sorting out options available to us as we move ahead.

It is my intention here to help each husband and wife understand — and, I hope, adopt as matters of conviction — some principles for forming character in their children. All of these principles derive from the successful experiences of other couples I have known well. These approaches toward successful character-formation should become clearer in the serious questions and issues I propose for each couple to think about and discuss, not only with each other but also among friends who share their concerns.

Exploring issues together like this is important for one overriding reason: the single most significant trait of successful parents is *unity of mind and will* in dealing with their children. Each child has only one mind and only one conscience, and therefore needs *one unified and coherent set of directions coming from both parents.* Parental disunity, especially in matters of discipline and moral principles, can lead to frictions in family life and a distortion in the children's character formation. On the other hand, mutual agreement in fundamental questions of family life nearly always promotes harmonious, steady growth in the children's moral development.

When a husband and wife discuss strategic questions together, they can also preempt some of the problems common to families when the children later grow to adolescence. Now, while the children are still young, the parents can address any differences in attitudes and expectations that may lie beneath the surface, covered over (though subtly perceptible from time to time) in the frantic swirl of daily family life. Now is the time, not later when the children are teenagers, to address these differences realistically, to secure experienced advice if necessary, and to resolve matters by compromise.

In short, the parents' unity of purpose and principles is vital for the children's long-term happiness. It is my hope that parents who think through and talk out the issues in this handbook will thus be better able to understand and support each other — so that their children will grow strong in a home environment of confident, harmonious parental leadership.

As you will see, many of the questions and issues here are open-ended. A husband and wife may not have had enough experience to find a satisfactory answer, at least not easily. This leads us to consider the other great need that parents face today: experienced advice.

Young parents today have to deal with what is, historically speaking, an unusual family situation. Broadly speaking, practically all parents everywhere have an occasional need for practical, experienced advice from other parents. Mothers and fathers throughout history and in all social circumstances, it seems, have needed to turn to others — respected relatives or friends — to get advice and, very frequently, real encouragement.

Children, of course, do not come into the world with a set of instructions. And conscientious parents in every generation wonder, and often worry, about the same sorts of questions: How much discipline is enough? Where do you draw the line between what is acceptable and what is not? How do you best handle this problem with this type of child? And so on, with dozens of similar issues and concerns.

The problem today is that parents are typically quite isolated from relatives and lifelong family friends. Parents and grown siblings usually live some distance apart. Neighbors come and go. Clergymen are frequently busy, even overwhelmed, with handling serious "problem cases" among families with out-of-control adolescents. What, then, is a normal young couple with normal concerns (so far) to do? Where can they turn for confidence-building advice and practical suggestions?

In my experience, they do not have to go very far.

If you are seriously concerned about the moral upbringing of your children in today's society, you have much company. Very many young parents, many more than you might think, share your earnest desires to raise children right, to prepare the youngsters to withstand and overcome the serious dangers that lie ahead in their lives — drug and alcohol abuse, sexual permissiveness, "peer pressures," marital breakup, depression and purposelessness, even suicide. (Of the children in U.S. grammar schools today, about 10% will have serious problems with alcohol or other drugs, and about one-half will be divorced.)

Among the people you know even casually — neighbors, fellow parishioners, parents of your children's friends, co-workers — you can expect to find some other parents who share your moral convictions and your concerns. If you inquire around, you will find them. This, at least, has been the experience of a great many young parents I have known. I would venture to say this is truer today than it was 10 or 20 years ago.

It is my hope that this handbook, aside from its use by husband and wife at home, can also serve to bring like-minded parents together to discuss these questions and issues as a group. In my experience, when parents meet informally in small groups to discuss the matters in this handbook, several things happen. First, a great deal of experienced advice and insight come to light, especially if the group includes some older, "veteran" parents. Questions give rise to very practical details, thus providing the tactical "how" answers that the handbook points to. Secondly, parents grow in confidence. It is helpful to see that other parents have shared many of the same problems and have managed, somehow, to cope with them successfully. Confidence is contagious, and it characterizes every successful set of parents I have known. Moreover, parents come to see an important truth: there are many ways of raising children successfully, and the only really great mistake is neglect. As long as you are trying to raise your children right, and keep coming back to elemental principles (like those in this book),

14

you can be at least reasonably confident of your ultimate success. Finally, these parents often become close friends. Sharing moral principles and an overriding commitment to all your children's lifelong happiness forms a solid basis for really deep friendship — a parental peer-support that, in itself, builds confidence enormously.

If you stop to think about it, this overall approach — clarifying one's convictions, forming goals for the children's growth in character, getting detailed advice from relatives and friends, relying on support from one's spouse and close friends — is historically a normal and natural way of strengthening the family and raising children successfully. The format approximates, in the jumbled social circumstances of our era, the way that parents have grown in knowledge and confidence about family life for centuries. Today's parents, more than ever before, have to work at acquiring insights and experienced advice. But the results in family life, today as in past ages, are well worth the effort. We have one chance, and one only, to raise our children well.

* * *

Let me say some things here about the handbook's organization. I have tried to keep it as simple and schematic as possible, outlining ideas succinctly and numbering them for easy reference in group discussion. As a result, the book is rather short and (I hope) tightly packed with thought-provoking questions and issues. The fleshing out of these — through examples, illustrations, personal experiences, and the like — should take place in the discussions, first between husband and wife and then among friends meeting as a group. In short, the handbook's contents should provoke the kind of thinking and idea-exchange that lead to practical insights and helpful suggestions.

The first chapter in the handbook gives a broad overview of character, and it begins by exploring some premises and assumptions about how character is normally formed in children. Before beginning discussion of the book's contents, it is important for husband and wife, or groups of couples, to see to what extent they agree on these assumptions and various definitions of terms.

Chapter One then proceeds to consider the components of character as such. For this I have used the seven classic virtues (inner strengths) of Christian civilization: faith, hope, charity, prudence, justice, fortitude, and temperance. I also describe the corresponding weaknesses associated with the absence of each virtue. A great many parents have found this framework helpful for evaluating their children's growth in character.

Chapter Two, much longer, describes the characteristics I have found most common among successful parents, the traits most often exhibited by people who have managed to raise their children well. I think you will find these items to be thought-provoking, stimulating, and encouraging.

There is no set formula for husband and wife, or groups of couples, to discuss the contents of these first two chapters. You can follow whatever format appeals to you. As I think you will see, the contents of each lend themselves to personal reflection, examination of family circumstances, and expression of opinions. Such has been people's experience.

Chapter Three takes a different approach to considering character-formation. I have listed a number of "life-lessons" that I believe young people need to learn, somehow, before they turn 21. This is another way of looking at the virtues — internalized truisms that all of us learn, or should learn, as we grow through childhood and adolescence. We learn these through word, example, and practice.

What we aim for here is that parents and group participants reach into their personal memories and explain how they learned each of these life-lessons. Among these many first-person accounts of experience, you should find a great number of useful tips and ideas. When all is said and done, there is no substitute for experience.

The final chapter consists of 16 broad "strategy-issues" dealing with family life. Each has statements and questions designed to provoke reflective discussion. As you will see, they are drawn from principles and observations in previous sections of the book. Some, no doubt, you will find more helpful than others; but I hope you find them all useful in defining your own convictions, setting your family-life goals, and looking more hopefully to your children's future as mature, responsible men and women.

* * *

Finally, here are some tips on organizing an informal discussion group with other couples:

• Keep it simple. Anywhere from three to eight couples seems to work best, the number of people who can comfortably meet in a living room or small conference room. Be sure, if possible, to include "veterans," some older parents with grown children — people whose experience is valuable.

• Keep it reasonably structured, with a format agreed upon by participants beforehand. Arrange to meet for a "block" of sessions, anywhere from five to ten meetings that will cover certain sections of the book; this is all that people commit themselves to, and they thus can diplomatically discontinue if they wish. After this "block" of meetings, take a couple of months break and then begin another. In any event, do not count on an open-ended commitment; there should be a clear cut-off point. Monthly or biweekly meetings seem to work best, and Friday or Saturday night from 8:00 to 9:30 or so works well for most couples.

• Keep it light. Count on having light refreshments during or after each meeting. Bear in mind that couples today need encouragement and friendship as well as practical advice; consequently, strive to make the discussion lively and enjoyable for everyone. In this, as in family life itself, try to be serious of purpose but light in touch.

1

CHARACTER

Discussion of the issues that follow in this book should proceed most clearly if we begin with a commonly shared understanding about the formation of children's character and conscience. Therefore, do you *agree,* or *disagree,* or *agree with certain qualifications* with each of the following statements?

1. To grow up as mature, responsible men and women who live by Christian principles, children must acquire an internalized understanding of certain truths about reality — both earthly and supernatural reality.

2. Children must learn these truths princi-

pally in family life, and *then* from school and society.

3. They learn these truths by

- *word:* what is repeatedly told to them by people whom they respect;

- *example:* what they *witness* practiced in the lives of parents and others whom they respect, both adults and peers;

- *practice:* what they repeatedly do, or are led to do, in the course of everyday life, both at home and in school.

4. Family and social circumstances have changed so much in recent years that middle-class children are frequently *not learning* these truths as they physically mature. Children thus often grow into their 20's with a distorted understanding of reality. They remain with the weaknesses of childhood; they are irresolute, self-centered, irresponsible, self-indulgent, and irreligious. Their lives are harmed because of childhood *neglect* — they have lacked *word, example,* and *practice.*

5. Word alone does not seem to be enough. It seems that children can receive plenty of verbal instruction as they grow up — religion lessons, stern admonitions, lectures, warn-

ings, and the like — and still fail to learn these life-lessons. What they have missed, apparently, are the other crucial elements: example and personal practice.

6. There are no fool-proof formulas for successful upbringing. Each child is different, and each human being is essentially a mystery. Nevertheless, generally speaking the premises mentioned above seem to be universally valid. Each child must have some sort of instruction, some sort of example to emulate, and some sorts of practice in the human and supernatural strengths of character. What these will be may differ for each family and even for each child. In any event, what is fatal for the children's maturity is *neglect*. In the long run, what seems to "work" in nearly all cases are two things: first, the parents' *determination* to raise their children toward responsible adulthood; and secondly, a conscious *effort* to teach the children through word, example, and practice.

7. Therefore, as long as parents have this clear determination and this commitment to teach (by whatever detailed methods), they have reason to be *confident*. Their confident optimism is, in fact, essential to the success of their efforts. The children need to see this

confidence, for they tend (as all of us do) to admire and imitate confident people. An attitude of fearfulness or unreasonable anxiety in the parents is a poor basis for forming character-strengths in children. Nobody respects fear.

8. In the final analysis, the children are ultimately in God's hands. There is only so much parents can do with their children, and the rest remains in God's Providence — which is itself a source of parental confidence. All God asks of parents, when they come before his judgment, is that they be able to say, "We tried our very best...."

Having looked at these assumptions about how character is formed in children, broadly speaking, let us now look more closely at character itself.

Character may generally be considered as the sum total of certain virtues (to use the classical term) that inhere within an individual's personality. The term *virtue* means simply an inner-directed and habitual strength of mind and will. Virtues are what make us admire certain people. (Doesn't all respect derive somehow from a perception of strength?)

Our civilization has long thought of seven

virtues as critical to mature Christian adulthood. Three of these are called supernatural virtues, dealing with our relationship before God: faith, hope, and charity. The other four have been called the cardinal virtues: prudence, justice, fortitude, and temperance. In today's common terminology, we would refer to these four by other names: sound judgment, a sense of responsibility, personal toughness, and self-control. (All other character strengths — such as industriousness, perseverance, courage, savvy — derive from these four fundamental powers of mind and will.)

Whatever we call these strengths, they are very real. We know them when we see them in people, and we are dismayed by their absence.

The collective experience of mankind is that parents have to teach all seven of these strengths. Mothers and fathers have to teach sound judgment as much as faith, and self-control as much as charity. Knowing the truths of one's faith and the common Christian prayers is vitally important, of course. But so, too, is learning to read critically, to carry out duties faithfully, to ignore temptations to laziness, to recognize sloppiness in thinking, to do without luxuries, to put up quietly with hardships and disappointment, and so on.

Experience over the last three or four decades has been that children's lessons in catechism and piety cannot effectively survive through adulthood *unless* the children have *also* learned to be discriminating thinkers, responsible doers, tough-minded and self-reliant people of action.

All of this means that parents must make a deliberate effort to teach their children all seven of these strengths, and to teach these to the point where they become part of the children's nature. This is a great challenge, but it is do-able. The most successful parents have done it, as we shall see later.

Let's take a look at these virtues/strengths one by one. All seven of them form a useful framework for thinking about the children's growth in character.

Faith: Belief in God and in all that he has revealed about himself and mankind. This includes an understanding of who we are (beloved children of God), where we are ultimately headed (heaven or hell), and what we are called to carry out here on earth (service to him by service to others, starting with one's own family and friends). In a real sense, faith is a matter of seeing every aspect of our life as God sees it, to be conscious of being always in his presence. From another perspective, it is a sense of *priorities* in life — that faithfulness to God's will comes *first,* ahead of everything else whatsoever.

Hope: Belief that God will give us the means for our salvation, and that he watches over all our affairs with loving Providence. Hope is the overriding *confidence* in God's all-knowing, all-loving, and all-powerful protection. For a person with the supernatural strength of hope, no hardship or setback or calamity is totally overwhelming — because, for a conscientious son or daughter of God, all things work together for the good. The Christian symbol of hope is the anchor, the tie that holds us securely through the storms of life.

Charity: Love for God, sincerely beloved as a Father and all-forgiving Friend. Here the question is one of *priority* and *intimacy.* The love for God comes absolutely first, ahead even of one's own life — as was the case with the Christian martyrs, who surrendered everything good in life rather than offend God, their first love. This love for God is deepened, made internal in mind and heart, through prayer and personal sacrifice. In everyday terms, it means shunning any and all allurements that could lead to sin, an offense against God. The great moral choices in life, therefore, come down to one fundamental option: *self or God,* and sometimes *self or others* (for the sake of God).

Sound judgment (Prudence): The acquired ability to accurately assess people, events, issues, ideas. The ability to evaluate human affairs in terms of causes and future implications. A commitment to truth. An ability to recognize hokum and lies when we see them. To look at this strength another way, it is the power of discrimination, the ability to make the important *distinctions* in life — truth from falsehood, good from evil, fact from opinion, objective reality from subjective feelings, the important from the trivial, the eternal from the transitory, and so on. A well-formed conscience belongs here. Conscience is an intellectual framework for evaluating rightness; it is not a bundle of intuitive sentiments.

Responsibility (Justice): Giving others what is due to them as a matter of right. (The word *duty* comes from "due.") The habitual understanding that the existence of others' rights imposes obligations on us. It is what children call "fairness" — one of the strongest and earliest-developed moral senses in children. (You can frequently correct children successfully by appealing to their sense of "fairness.") Combined with the virtue of sound judgment, and especially sound conscience, it is an habitual understanding of the interplay between rights and duties — between authority and responsibility — in our dealings with family and society, and above all in our dealings with God. It therefore implies *respect* for others' dignity, freedom, and feelings. It also entails fortitude and self-control (see below) in *acting* to carry out one's duties for the sake of others' happiness and welfare. (At some point children must learn that love is not a sentiment; real love is the willingness and ability to undergo hardship for the sake of others' welfare.)

Toughness (Fortitude): Courage, persistence, perseverance, "guts" — the ability to endure or overcome pain, inconvenience, disappointment, for the sake of some higher good (for example, one's duty to God and others). It is the habitual power to either *solve* problems or *put up* with them. It is the ability to override one's fears and ignore one's feelings. (Courage is perfectly compatible with personal fearfulness; a courageous person does what's right *despite* his or her anxieties. All children must learn this, especially by example and practice.)

Self-control (Temperance): Related to personal toughness, this is the ability to dominate one's passions, appetites, and "feelings" for the sake of a higher good. It is mastery over our lower inclinations, including the ever-present temptations toward laziness. It is "being on top of life," in control of events, living as a self-reliant "self-starter." Clearly it is one of the indispensable qualities of leadership, one of the character strengths we admire most in people. What we think of as "class" in people seems directly related to their habitual power of self-restraint, of self-mastery. Temperance is the foundation (along with charity) of courtesy, habitual good manners.

It should be evident, even from this brief overview of the virtues, that these traits of character constitute the inner core of what we most admire in the finest people we have known. They are the traits that conscientious parents earnestly want to see take shape inside their children as the youngsters grow to adulthood.

To look at it another way, parents who reflect about the future of their children would strongly hope to see these traits in their children's future *spouses*. Considering all seven of these strengths as a frame of reference, what sort of young man would you hope your daughter will someday marry? And what sort of woman should be the future wife of your son? (For some reason, parents find it easier to describe ideal future sons-in-law and daughters-in-law than they do to describe their own grown children. Perhaps the "ideal son-in-law" would be a useful model for one's own grown son, and the same for the daughter.)

This consideration of the seven classic strengths of character might become clearer if we consider their opposites. The weaknesses in these areas are all the more evident and even glaring around us. Any teacher could think of dozens of young people who fit such descriptions; so could employers, divorce lawyers, and marriage counselors. A young adult with the weaknesses described below is every conscientious parent's nightmare as a prospective future spouse for his or her children.

What are these principle character weaknesses, corresponding to the virtues we've just listed?

Faithlessness: Given the fundamental option between God and self (as we've seen before), the faithless person lives solely for self. God's existence and moral precepts form no serious part of his or her life-vision. Man, therefore, is seen — at least in practice — from a materialistic viewpoint. That is, man is considered to be a mere thing, an object, a pleasure-driven "consumer." One's self-centeredness is supported and rationalized by religious skepticism and moral relativism. In practical terms, only the law acts as an effective constraint on actions; whatever the law permits is, *ipso facto,* permissible. (And the law allows for easy divorce.)

Despair: The absence of confidence in God, and eventually in anything else, especially in the face of serious crisis. It is a sense of hopelessness, helplessness, and a sort of shapeless loneliness when coming up against life's inevitable sorrows and disappointments. Among hard-core materialists, this despair acts as a thematic counterpoint to headlong pleasure-seeking; the mind flits back and forth between joy (often from drugs or alcohol) and loneliness. If unchecked, it can lead to depression and suicide. (Question: Why is the suicide rate among young people almost directly proportional to their family income — and yet, among permanently crippled paraplegics it is practically zero?)

Egoism: The opposite of charity. It habitually puts other goods before God or the welfare of others: pleasure, honors, comfort, convenience, power, money. Relationships to others are based on usefulness or transitory sentiments, not respect for inherent rights and desire for others' happiness. (When marriage is based on self-centered sentiments, it can rapidly and easily break apart. The current length for marriages in the United States is slightly under seven years.)

Immature Judgment: Muddled thinking. Having one's judgment over-influenced by sentiment, self-interest, and fashionable "consensus." It is essentially the mental operations of young children — fuzzy, over-emotional, uncritical, undiscriminating — but without children's natural curiosity. It is a smugly passive ignorance, rather easily swayed by appeals to vanity, conformity, sentimentality, and appetites — the standard, time-tested techniques of persuasion used by demagogues and advertisers. It is the habitual disinclination to ask the question "Why?" It is a lack of serious interest in either the past or the future. It values people and events in terms of amusement and entertainment; the only thing taken really seriously is the *self*.

Irresponsibility: This is a preoccupation with one's own rights, comfort, feelings, and a corresponding disregard for the welfare and sensibilities of others. It is an exclusive concern for one's own interests, often rationalized as "my rights." It is essentially the mind-set of a spoiled child carried over into later life. In the broad sense, it is a relentless drive for power.

Softness: This is an habitual tendency to avoid difficulty, to quit, to escape. It is an inability to solve tough problems or to live with tough situations. It is clearly one of the hallmarks of a "consumer" mentality. Personal softness weakens all other aspects of children's moral formation; without fortitude, children cannot seem to bring themselves to do what they know is right. Conscience turns into wishful thinking and eventually it can atrophy through disuse. (Question: To what extent is divorce caused by young people's inability to endure the normal, reasonable frictions inherent in any close human relationship?)

Self-indulgence: The opposite of temperance. An intemperate person puts no reasonable limits on his or her passions, appetites, whims — and sees no reason to do so, except perhaps for physical health. Intemperate people turn wants into needs. During adolescence, they are powerfully attracted to drugs, sex, alcohol, and other physical stimulants. Whatever conscience they may have formed since infancy is overshadowed and then dominated by their desires, and often rationalized away. Typically, such young people have a weakly developed spiritual sense — religious practice withers away, and in many cases there is little appreciation for artistic beauty. Their thinking is characterized by emotionalism, "spontaneity," and coarse humor. Speech is often punctuated with vulgarity. If they are attracted to a religion, it must be emotionally exciting but otherwise undemanding; it must give religious satisfaction without asking sacrifice.

When we look at these weaknesses of character, we are struck by one common thread among them (except perhaps with despair): They are vestiges of childhood.

Let's be frank about it. Small children —
despite their capacity for innocent goodness
— are essentially self-preoccupied little crea-
tures who are wholly given over to gratifying
their appetites and imposing their will upon
others. They are seldom innately grateful or
cooperative. Their thinking is fuzzy and
undiscriminating, strongly affected by
self-interested emotions.

In short, children come into this world
with weaknesses of character, and these
weaknesses must be turned into strengths as
the children grow to physical adulthood. This
does not happen naturally and unaided. It
must be made to happen by the efforts of parents and other responsible adults: teachers,
coaches, clergy, older siblings, and sometimes
also the children's peers.

This seems to be one of those truths that
are so obvious they are often overlooked: If
children do not learn character-strengths —
by word, example, and repeated practice —
then they retain the weaknesses of childhood
well into adolescence and even adulthood.
Though such young people may attain
advanced degrees and professional skills,
they remain self-centered, pleasure-driven,
irresponsible. Their adult life may seem like
that of high-powered adolescence; their

income is essentially just "spending money." They are poorly prepared for the sacrifices intrinsic to married life, and marriage falls easily apart. In extreme cases, these young narcissists care neither for their parents nor for their own children. (In the U.S., more than a million women a year pay a doctor to kill their unborn child.)

Clearly, in a great many families today this process of character formation is not happening.

The reasons for this neglect are too complex to discuss in detail here. But to help focus our thinking and discussion, perhaps we can at least outline some of the more significant ones. The question, then, is this: What elements in the life of families today could account for the *absence* of character formation in the children's upbringing? The following seem to stand out:

1. *Children are not really needed at home.* Unlike in previous ages of history, even up until quite recently, children do not have much to contribute to the family's well-being. Their powers of performing meaningful work are not really necessary either to the family or to society. Since work-performance enhances responsibility, and therefore one's sense of self-worth, the children are missing

out in the practice of exercising their strengths. There is generally little or no experience with adult-level responsibilities.

2. *Parents, and especially fathers, give little example of strengths.* Children today hardly ever witness their parents work, especially their fathers. The virtues that fathers exercise in carrying out responsible work — judgment, responsibility, toughness, self-control — are typically out of the children's vision. Children see their fathers mostly in a leisure context, relaxing around the house or just watching television. Indeed, many children have no idea whatever of what their father does for a living.

3. *Television has replaced conversation and reading.* Until the invention of television, conversation at home managed to compensate considerably for the children's separation from their parents during the day; children grew to know a lot about their parents' lives and thinking. In our time, two or three hours a day of television sensory-stimulation has crowded out conversation almost entirely. (By some estimates, parents and children now converse for less than 20 minutes a day.) Reading, which used to be a significant window on adult reality, is today

minimal or non-existent.

4. *Entertainers have replaced heroes.* By definition, a hero is one who embodies outstanding strengths of character. Every culture in history has presented children with heroes to emulate — people who did great deeds in the fulfillment of responsibilities. Today, children's thinking (often led by the parents' example) is dominated by figures from the entertainment industry. To what extent do comedians and "celebrities" teach young people about sound judgment, responsibility, toughness, and self-control?

5. *Adolescents have become an artificial leisure class.* The age between 13 and 23, which formerly was the beginning of adult-level responsibility, has become a commercially exploitable culture all its own. Adolescents have the freedom and powers of adulthood (usually more physical freedom than their parents) together with the irresponsibility of childhood, a dangerous combination. The teen culture is not centered (to say the least) on the acquisition of virtues. Rather, it gives several years' practice in self-indulgence and emotional excess. The teen years seem to be one last fling at life rather than a preparation for it. Like other

leisure classes in history, adolescents today function principally as consumers; they spend unearned income largely on leisure pursuits.

6. *Religious sacrifice has markedly declined.* Prosperity usually brings with it a decline of religious belief and sacrificial practice. Riches tend to smother the great existential questions — What is man? What are we here for? To Whom do we answer for the way we live? — and religious practice becomes routine custom, easily dispensable. Children raised in this environment thus do not see their parents living as responsible to a higher internalized ethic. God lives in church, not in the hearts and minds of the family. There is thus a minimal sense of our answerability to anything except the law and social convention. (So, what happens when the law and social convention condone immoral behavior? What then serves as a binding force for an upright life?)

7. *Society has come to see character as something to be maintained in children, not formed.* This is a subtle and complex set of attitudes that has arisen over the last several generations, affecting large segments of the educational establishment and of society

as a whole.

The fundamental notion is this: Children are born good, and their upbringing should therefore aim to preserve or maintain this inherent goodness against the environment's corruptive influences as the children grow to adulthood. Evil is seen, therefore, as something entirely extrinsic to the children's nature, something against which children need to be protected as long as possible. (Many readers will recognize this notion as originating with the social critic Jean Jacques Rousseau.)

This approach to dealing with children is deeply rooted because it is attractive for a number of reasons. There is no question that children come into the world with many beautiful qualities. They are naturally curious, for instance, and open to learning. They are also simple, trusting, and charmingly (sometimes embarrassingly) frank. And, of course, there is no question that children can be corrupted by elements of the environment.

What has followed from this viewpoint is the way children are dealt with by schools and by large numbers of parents. Schools seem oriented toward cultivating childhood rather than preparing for adulthood. To grow up well, therefore, the children need to be

41

kept busy, to have their good feelings fulfilled, to "feel good about themselves," to be spontaneous and "creative."

There is nothing inherently wrong with these generalizations, of course, and children do have needs along these lines. What is missing, however, is the notion of *building virtues* in the children, forming *habitual strengths of character* to replace the children's inherent weaknesses. Children do not come into the world with sound judgment, a sense of responsibility, personal toughness, and self-control. And as for the religious strengths — faith, hope, and charity — the experience of the last 2,000 years is that each generation of children has to be *missionized* in Christian values, or the kids will grow up faithless.

In other words, and as people have believed for centuries, the acquisition of character does not just happen as the children grow up. It must be made to happen. In fact, the collective experience of mankind in this matter has been quite straightforward: If children are not deliberately formed in character-strengths, then they grow up to be larger versions of what they were in childhood. They remain self-indulgent, irresponsible, egoistic, and immature in judgment. Though they may attain a certain professional and monetary success, their personal lives may be a wreck.

2

SUCCESSFUL PARENTS: A PROFILE

Successful parents are, simply speaking, parents who raise successful children. That is, they are fathers and mothers whose children grow up, often rather quickly, to become men and women of strong conscience and character, young adults who habitually exercise the seven virtues we have described. These young adults honor their parents, as God commands all of us to do, by adopting their parents' principles, making them their own, and then passing them on to their own children intact.

It is important for parents today to realize that this success with one's children is possible. A great number of parents, despite their own shortcomings and the inroads of a tough environment, do manage to raise their children well. Young couples today, therefore, have plenty of reason for hope.

What is striking about these successful people is their diversity. Temperament and "talent" do not seem to be crucially important to effective character-building. Some successful parents are energetic extroverts; others are quiet and mild-mannered. Some seem to sense immediately what needs to be done with their children in a host of situations; others, far more numerous, have serious concerns and questions and so they seek experienced advice. Some are home-centered, though not to a fault; others are busy in professional and social affairs, but not to excess.

Experience shows that all of these successful parents, without exception, have personal faults and sometimes personal doubts about their effectiveness at home. All have occasionally experienced disappointment and even exasperation with their children's attitudes and behavior, especially during adolescence. Nevertheless, these parents manage to triumph. In the long run, sometimes the very long run, their children grow up well.

Despite the many differences in temperament and approaches among these successful people, they seem to have several traits in common — several attitudes, approaches, and patterns of behavior that contribute significantly to their children's upbringing in character. It is these common traits that we want to discuss briefly here. They are as follows:

1. *Unity:* The parents work as a unified team. They thoroughly support each other in the common endeavor of raising the children well. (Many parents have told me that this unity is one of the two most important elements, the other being religious convictions.) Though the parents inevitably have differences of opinion in many matters, they manage to agree — to smooth over differences through compromise — in matters relating to the children's discipline. They realize that they, as a couple, must present a united front to the children when teaching them right from wrong. Each child has only one mind and one conscience, and therefore needs one consistent set of directions emanating from both parents. Clever, manipulative children can take advantage of disunity between their parents, playing off one against the other. Successful parents simply do not permit this to happen.

2. *Mutual respect:* Related to the unity described above, each parent frequently *shows* the children his or her respect for the other spouse. In the children's eyes, therefore, each parent is "boss" — both of them exercising the same authority, each in a different but complementary way. The children have no doubts that, in Dad's eyes, Mom is the absolutely number one person in his life. And similarly they see that, to Mom, Dad is a model of manly strength and leadership.

This relationship between the parents — where the spouse's welfare and happiness comes first, and then the children's — seems to teach the children an enormous amount *mainly by example.* This living example of respect, generosity, and self-sacrifice seems much more important than lectures, reprimands, and other verbal teaching. In fact, it forms the whole context for what the children are told; what is said serves to *draw the children's attention to what they see before them.*

Incidentally, psychological studies show that children's attitudes toward each parent directly mirror the other parent's attitudes. To the extent that each parent respects the other, and shows this, the children unconsciously adopt the same respect themselves. Thus, if a husband shows an apparent indif-

ference to his wife (and many do, unwittingly), he soon finds his children treating her
with sass. If a wife does not show respect for
her husband's moral leadership, the children
grow indifferent to his direction — and look
elsewhere for heroes to emulate.

**3. *Seeing children as adults-in-the-
making:*** Successful parents have a clear
idea that they are raising adults, not children. They frequently think of their children's future as men and women. Though
they understand and appreciate the weaknesses of children, they realize that the kids
need correction and leadership to grow up.
They know how to play with the children and
come down to their level of understanding;
but they do not *stay* there. They want to raise
the children up to their own level.

Consequently the children see them enjoy
living as adults, people of confident accomplishment.

None of this means, of course, that the
parents "rush" the kids to strive and compete
for its own sake, a common attitude today
among the selfishly ambitious. Kids need to
be kids. But the parents steadily encourage
their children to grow in judgment, responsibility, and perseverance — thus leading them
patiently toward self-reliant adulthood —

preferably before the children are out of their teens.

4. *Religious convictions:* Almost universally, the most successful parents take their religious convictions seriously, leading to sacrificial practice of one's faith. The parents personally teach and oversee the children's religious instruction. Prayer before meals, dressing well for church, giving ethical explanations in a God-centered way, celebrating Sunday and religious feasts, cordial regard for clergy and religious, generosity toward the church — all of these *show* the children that the parents see the family as dependent on God, grateful to him for his blessings.

The children witness, moreover, that the parents themselves are responsible to God, answerable to him for the way life is lived. This gives a reasonability to the ethical correction of the children, a *life-long* dimension to the guidance of right and wrong. Without this parental example (say, in religiously lukewarm homes), children can form the impression that right/wrong questions are only for children, that adulthood brings liberation from ethical constraints. Society, of course, reinforces this viewpoint; films are "for mature audiences only," and "under 17 not admitted" — the distinction between

49

right and wrong seemingly becoming merely a question of age.

5. *Discipline treated as strength-building not merely control:* Successful parents combine firmness with understanding; they treat their children the way God treats all of us. They lay down the law, but affectionately and with forgiveness. They hate the sin but love the sinner. They show their children that they love them enough to correct their faults, and thereby build strengths. They are thus neither harsh nor soft-hearted, neither tyrannical nor permissive — for both of these extremes are essentially self-centered.

Consistently, successful parents do not permit anything in family life that they do not approve of. Whether their "judgment calls" are correct or mistaken, the parents have no doubt of their right to make decisions for the children's welfare, and to make them stick.

Children raised this way come to see, sooner or later (sometimes not until adulthood), that all their parents' disciplinary efforts derive from their love and their spirit of sacrifice.

6. *A stress on responsibility as well as freedom:* Successful parents make each child feel *needed* at home. Each child is led to contribute some efforts, however small, toward making the home a successful team enterprise. "Chores" are not busy-work but confidence-building exercises in responsibility; thus *follow-through* in making sure they're completed is paramount. The children's contributions to the home life are thus real and appreciated. Successful parents *make praise as specific as blame.* (We tend to make praise general and vague, but to put blame in specifics — a mistake.) Children seem to thrive on this assessment; they need it to form a realistic appraisal of their self-worth and self-respect.

Incidentally, this inculcation of responsibility seems inherent and most effective in larger families, as might be expected. The children's help at home is genuinely needed, and the children seem to acquire maturity and self-control more quickly, along with a healthy self-confidence. Teachers can often easily spot children from a large family; such youngsters generally seem more imaginative and self-reliant. Parents who have four or more children often cannot provide much spending money or many gadgets in the home, but they seem to provide something more important to the children — an early-developed depth of character.

7. *Television kept under control:* Successful parents do not permit television or the other entertainment media to act as *rivals* for their children's respect and affection. They monitor and control what the family members watch at home. This is not done merely to *shield* the children (impossible in any event) but rather to express lessons of what is approved and what is not. Children thus see that the home is not open to persons and attitudes that offend the parents' principles.

Moreover, successful parents seem to realize that the children's time is too valuable to waste on mindless amusement. Children's minds are built to learn actively, not to be stroked passively by flitting sensations. Children need time for conversation and reading and healthy play, the age-old means by which children have learned about adult life in the world outside the family. (How often do you ever see anyone on television reading a book, or doing productive work, or praying? Television-viewing is so boring, in fact, that we almost never see anyone on TV actually watching TV.)

None of this means that successful parents necessarily eliminate television altogether. Rather, they teach the children by example how to exercise discrimination of judgment. They also teach, indirectly, that entertainment is something to be enjoyed in moderation; we can do with it or without it. Thus the children do not form a habit of being passively amused. Entertainment is viewed as a spice to life, not the main course.

8. *Frequent conversation with children:* Related to their control over television, keeping it to a minimum in family life, successful parents converse a lot with their children. They go out of their way, it seems, to know what is on their children's minds, and to let the kids know their own. Parents talk about their own experiences, their struggles and responsibilities (past and present), their convictions and principles, their life with their own parents (the kids' grandparents), the people whom they admire and why, their concerns for the children's future, their views on contemporary affairs and issues — in short, the whole range of their minds. Over time, this discussion leads to respect and affection among the children; the parents' values, clearly and calmly expressed, give a reasoned context for the parents' actions. The children learn *why* their parents act as they do in giving leadership to the family's life together.

There is simply no substitute for this knowledge gained through personal conversation. It is the bond for passing on spiritual values from one generation to another — the criteria for sound judgment and firm conscience, family continuity, family honor, family traditions. Tragically, in so many families today, this parent-to-children bond is shunted aside in favor of cartoons, game-shows, violent melodramas, rock entertainers and other prancing clowns. Small wonder that so many parents and children know so little about each other.

(Experience indicates that young people who successfully resist peer-pressures — that is, who emerge through adolescence with their parents' values intact — seem to have a common characteristic: they *know* their parents very well and they deeply *respect* them.)

9. *Discipline seen as worthwhile investment:* Finally, successful parents all seem to realize, at least intuitively, that they have one chance — and only one — to raise their children right. They know they have only the first 16 to 18 years of each child's life, and often less than this, to prepare that young person's earthly and eternal happiness. This is a very brief flash of time, and it

54

passes only once.

There is no time, therefore, to slack off or delay what needs to be taught *now*. Too much is at stake. A relentlessly determined effort — calling forth all of one's faith, mind, will, and strength — is urgently necessary, today more than ever. This struggle is inevitably tiring, but it is worth the sacrifice. And the example of this oftentimes heroic effort is itself formative for the kids.

When the children are grown and gone, then the parents can relax and enjoy the fruits of their labors — grown children, and then grandchildren, who are the delight of their lives.

Indeed, there seems to be a balancing economy, a sort of universal law in child-raising: you pay now, or you pay later. So many parents find this out the hard way. They practice comfortable neglect when the children are small, and then endure heart-breaking disappointment later, even tragedy. Successful parents will make any sacrifice now to keep this from happening. They seem to know that their children's future happiness, the very stability of their children's future marriage, everything depends on making sacrifices *now*, while the children are young enough to learn life's all-important lessons — a confident, persistent teaching of character-strengths through word, example, and repeated practice.

3

LIFE-LESSONS IN REALITY

IN THE PAGES that follow, we have compiled a set of life-lessons — some statements about reality, both human and supernatural — that each young person should learn, and indeed *must* learn, by the time he or she leaves the teen years behind. Under each of these statements there is a set of explanations or corollary ideas, with each phrased in the second person form ("you..."), as if given by parent to child. This collection of life-lessons is by no means exhaustive, of course; you and your spouse or friends could probably think of at least a dozen more. What we have here is just a beginning. It's an initial and (we hope) useful framework for *thinking* about what your children need to learn while they are growing up. As you can see, we are essentially working backward — proceeding from the projected "final product" (your children's future values and understanding about life) and considering what needs to be taught now to bring this about.

The basis for this consideration — as well as practical suggestions for effective teaching — comes from discussion based on *experience*. Individual couples, or groups of couples, or even groups of friends should take each of these life-lesson statements and reflect on one's personal experience with each of them. Consider each in light of the following questions:

1. How did I come to learn this lesson? What did my parents and other adults tell me about it, and under what circumstances? What *example* did I witness in the lives of my parents and other adults that drove this lesson home? What did my parents make me *do* in order to appreciate the truth of this lesson?

2. Given what I see and hear about in today's society, what keeps today's children from learning this lesson? What's happening

in today's family and social circumstances such that young people can grow up ignorant of this truth — and therefore out of touch with reality?

3. *If your children are already grown:* What did you do and say to teach your children this lesson about life? What seemed to work most effectively? If you had to do it again, what (if anything) would you change?

4. In practical terms, what can young parents do in today's circumstances to impart this lesson to their children? What might keep them from doing so? How can they overcome this obstacle?

It is hoped that focusing on each life-lesson like this, eliciting people's experiences and insights, will give each young couple several things: a clearer picture of the task at hand, some practical suggestions for family life, and a greater confidence in taking on the adventure of raising a family. Note, too, the great help that older "veteran" parents can contribute to this discussion.

1. *"Marriage is forever."*

A. Some people are called by God to live apostolic celibacy, to serve the Church and all souls in a special way. Everyone else is called to marriage, to serve the Church and all souls in *another* special way. When a society does not respect the sanctity of marriage, it does not respect the sanctity of apostolic celibacy. *Both* are holy vocations from God, calling for sacrifice and apostolic service.

B. Marriage is where all your upbringing, your character, your physical and spiritual and intellectual powers all come together. All of your education, in the broad sense, has been to prepare you for effective service to your spouse and children — and then to the society in which you and they will live.

C. Your spouse will have defects and personal shortcomings. This is a fact. Whatever you can't change, you must accept; your love can and must overshadow these personal defects. The respect that your children have for you and your spouse will depend on the loving respect that you have for each other, your defects notwithstanding.

D. Raising a family is an adventure. Like other great adventures, it has trials and setbacks, times of doubt and uncertainty, and moments of deep happiness and triumph. If God grants you the vocation to marriage, he calls you to an adventurous mission — to make your spouse happy through personal sacrifice, to work with him/her as a collaborative partner, to raise your children (God's gift to you) to become strong, competent, responsible men and women who habitually live by Christian principles.

2. ***"When you are a parent you will have one chance — and only one — to raise your children right."***

A. You must teach your children to have a firm conscience and a strong character. But you can't give what you haven't got.

B. Your children will learn these things through *word, example,* and *practice.* Your children must witness your strengths and convictions and conscience in action. If you rely only on words, they will consider you a weakling or a hypocrite. Through your neglect, you may wind up with children who are weak, unprincipled, and deeply troubled.

C. The greatest accomplishment in your life should be to work with your spouse to raise your children well — so that they become competent, responsible adults who live by Christian principles. All your other accomplishments in your job or social life are far less important than the character and conscience of your children.

D. The finest gift of gratitude you can give to us, your parents, is to *live by our principles* — to adopt them as your own and to pass them on intact to our grandchildren.

3. ***"Without a strong will-power, you'll never amount to anything."***

A. Will-power is the habitual ability to deny yourself, to say "no" to your feelings, to do your duty whether you feel like it or not.

B. All successful people in the world have had this quality. Such people have come from strikingly different social and economic backgrounds, but they have all had a capacity for sustained, concentrated effort, even in the face of serious obstacles.

C. People with will-power are generally confident, and therefore respected. If they are also genuinely considerate of others, they earn the devotion of people who know them. They are beloved and imitated. They have many close friends and a happy family life.

D.   Such people generally know that time is a *resource*. They *use* this resource, while others waste it.

E.   If you don't work to control events, then they control you.

F.   You can build will-power directly by *exercise*. Every time you do something despite your feelings, you grow just a little bit stronger.

G.   A person without will-power winds up with the look and the outlook of a victim.

4. "You are stronger than you think."

A. Your childhood and adolescence have been unrealistically easy. At some point, you will have to deal with challenging problems on your own. Don't let your fear overwhelm you.

B. Adversity and reasonable pressure bring out the best in us. Coping with tough problems helps us to clarify our strengths and shortcomings, and eventually it builds realistic confidence. The sooner this happens to you, the better.

C. Problems, therefore, are really opportunities for deepening character and building strengths of judgment and will. Almost everyone finds more strength than he or she suspected was there.

66

D. Fear in the face of adversity is nothing to be ashamed of; in fact, it's a sign of intelligence. (Only fools are never afraid.) What really counts is what we do in spite of our fears. Do we handle the problem as best we can...or do we run away? Escape accomplishes nothing inside of us; it only diminishes self-respect, and consequently the respect of others.

E. The sooner you learn to overcome fear — in a sense, to ignore it — the sooner you will grow up. The people closest to you later — spouse, children, friends, fellow workers — will depend on your ability to overcome your anxieties. They will depend on your strengths.

5. *"Comfort and convenience are only by-products of a successful life, not its purpose."*

A. A headlong pursuit of pleasure and an avoidance of pain at all costs lead, sooner or later, to disappointment and deep unhappiness for yourself and others.

B. A preoccupation with "self-fulfillment" and "being in touch with your feelings" results in frustration. The unhappiest people you will meet are those wholly preoccupied with themselves.

C. A life of comfort, peace, and security is rare in history and in most of the present world. It is not a state of nature. The prosperity we enjoy in the West is not "normal" and will not last indefinitely.

You must have a firm character to be prepared for any economic eventuality. Your future family will depend on it.

D.   Character is what you have left over when and if you go broke. It is you minus your material possessions.

6. *"Problems are inevitable, but we can turn them to our advantage."*

A. Some people see problems only as difficulties, things to be avoided at all costs. Other people see them as opportunities, a chance (which can't be avoided anyway) to grow in knowledge, personal strength, and service to others.

B. Sometimes a problem situation is miserable to go through but rather enjoyable to look back on. Some of the most interesting people you'll meet are those who have been through a lot of problems and emerged on top. Every great adventure in history was seen as an adventure afterwards, in retrospect; at the time, it seemed like a mass of problems. A confident problem-solving attitude is critical to success in life.

C. A relatively hassle-free existence is, in the last analysis, quite dull. Men and women with an escapist mentality are usually boring people.

D. Parents who solve all their children's problems are depriving them of the strength, and ultimately the happiness that comes with confidence. We, your parents, want to direct you, not manage you. By making your life a little bit harder, we are making you stronger. The sooner you learn to solve problems, or just live with them, the sooner you will become a responsible adult.

7. "Respect is the key to most significant human relationships."

A. Real friendship is based on respect, not just warm sentiments. The deepest friendships arise between people who greatly respect each other's character.

B. Familiarity is the outer-shell appearance of friendship, but without the underlying respect. Sooner or later, the absence of respect leads to contempt. (Hence: "Familiarity breeds contempt.")

C. Real friendship brings out the best in people.

D. Good manners are the way we show respect for other people's rights and dignity. Since living good manners takes strength, we thereby gain people's respect. (Respect always derives from perception of strength.) In other words, when you show respect to others, you gain their respect in turn.

E. A young adult who does not show good manners marks himself or herself as self-centered and immature.

F. Everyone in authority deserves special respect. The responsibility that he or she bears for our welfare is heavy and often seriously burdensome. People in legitimate authority, therefore, deserve courtesy and considerateness, especially in public.

G. The elderly also deserve being treated with refined courtesy. They are the people who built the society that we enjoy. They paid the taxes, fought the wars, kept our government and society intact through extremely difficult times. They have done much for all of us, and we honor them with gratitude for what they have left us — so easily taken for granted.

8. "Respect is more important than popularity, and it's harder to win."

A. You can get many people to like you somewhat just by being amusing. But don't confuse this sentiment with friendship or high regard. People enjoy clowns — but they don't trust them or follow them. A sidekick is, by definition, just an accomplice in play. Do you want people to think of you as a sidekick or a friend?

B. Real friendship and leadership will come to you when you've won people's respect. People will not merely like you. They will admire you and love you. Everything depends on respect, and this depends on your character.

C. Respect is always associated with strength. Respect comes from:

- sincere religious convictions and ethical principles
- considerateness and good manners (Adults always respect kids who show real courtesy.)
- professionalism: working to high standards, whether you feel like it or not
- virtues: sound judgment, a sense of responsibility, toughness, self-control
- personal integrity: where your intentions, your word, and your actions are all one
- being serious in purpose but light in touch: taking your responsibilities seriously, but not yourself.

D. If you're true to your convictions, you may suffer a temporary setback in popularity. But in the long run, you will win people's admiration. A few people will envy you and bear malice toward you, for your life will be a reproach to them; the rest of the people who know you will deeply admire you.

E. But whether you're admired or not, remember this: Only God's judgment is really important.

9. "Everybody is a package deal; nobody's perfect."

A. Everybody: parents, brothers and sisters, teachers, friends, bosses, your future spouse.

B. Consequently, if you look for defects in people, you'll always find them. Most people who harp about other people's faults are almost always really dissatisfied with themselves. Unconsciously they try to boost their own egos by tearing other people down. Confident and realistic people don't behave this way; they tend to see people as they are — a "package deal" of strengths and shortcomings — and they appreciate the good they see.

C. You can grow up sooner by looking for other people's strengths (everybody has some strengths) and by trying to imitate them.

D. Charity doesn't consist of giving away old clothes. It means having compassionate understanding for people. If some people pose a problem for you, try to see their problem from their point of view. Doing this habitually takes you out of childish self-concern and gives you genuine maturity of judgment.

E. Children are basically self-centered. Mature adults are other-centered. There are three stages of growing up:
- Child: "What can you do for me?"
- Adolescent: "Let me do it for myself."
- Mature adult: "What can I do for you?"

F. Hard feelings between people of fundamentally good will are almost always caused by misunderstanding. Remember this when you find yourself quarreling with someone whom you like and respect. And you can do much good as a "peacemaker," if you help quarreling friends (or spouses) to reach an understanding and a reconciliation.

G. If you're really serious about solving the world's problems, then start with yourself. Give people the benefit of the doubt. Shun gossip and backbiting at all costs. Work to elect public officials who share your principles.

H. If you work to grow in strength of character (judgment, responsibility, toughness, self-control), you will be a better parent, a better spouse, a better citizen, a better worker. Work on this betterment and you'll find yourself overlooking other people's faults.

10. "If responsibility and authority are out of balance, the result is trouble."

A. Freedom, authority, rights, "choice," "options" — all these terms really mean the same thing: power.

B. Outside of the youngest childhood, freedom relates directly to some responsibility — that is, to one's own or other people's welfare.

C. Small childhood is a period of irresponsible freedom. Over time, each child can and must take on responsibilities proportionate to his growing freedoms/powers. Giving too much freedom to young people, and not enough responsibility, can lead to protracted immaturity, lack of self-control, and even tragedy.

80

D. Everybody, young and old, needs freedom and responsibility to be in balance. Young people who can't handle responsibility adequately must have their freedom proportionately restricted; otherwise they can hurt themselves and others.

E. Since the responsibilities of parenthood are serious, then the authority of parents must be substantial. Parental responsibility (and therefore authority) does not end until the children can and do take responsibility for their own lives.

11. "Morality does not depend on majority vote or on age."

A. Right and wrong derive from man's nature and man's relation to God. Some things are wrong, no matter what the majority of people think. Throughout history, there have been plenty of serious evils that have been widely accepted by most people in society.

B. To be popular is not so important as being right. If you try hard to live an upright, chaste, and honorable life, you will probably find yourself "different" from others. To be honorable, therefore, takes personal courage and toughness.

C. Similarly, some activities are wrong for

everyone, no matter what the age. You do not shed your conscience or moral responsibility when you turn 18.

D. We all answer to God ultimately for the way we have lived. He is merciful but he is also just. It is his judgment that counts, not that of our peers.

E. Foster a spirit of gratitude to God. It is the basis for piety and an upright life. Those who see life as a gift on loan are the ones who enjoy it most — no matter what others say about them.

12. "You can't believe everything you read."

A. From childhood, we tend to form the attitude that whatever appears in print is authoritative — that is, almost certainly truthful and accurate.

B. But books and magazine articles and newspaper accounts are written by people. All of these people, being human beings, are capable of making mistakes. Moreover, some of them are biased in their judgments and do not share our principles. (Some, for example, honestly believe that man is merely a kind of clever animal, and that morality is just a social convention.) Professional writers are often highly skilled at presenting opinions convincingly, as if their positions were unassailable truth.

C. To read critically and intelligently requires several things:
- knowing your own principles
- being able to distinguish fact from opinion
- recognizing emotional appeals when you see them.

D. A person who gives uncritical assent to the written word is a carnival-salesman's dream. There is such a thing as a healthy skepticism.

E. As someone once said: You should always maintain an open mind, but not so open that your brains fall out.

13. "Fame is no longer connected with personal greatness."

A. Fame used to accompany personal heroism. People were widely known and admired for their character and accomplishments. Thus a famous person was usually a great man or woman, someone who had earned wide esteem. This is no longer true.

B. A whole industry has made it possible for dishonorable people to be widely honored. Skilled professionals can bring great fame to people who have done nothing to deserve it. This is why "celebrities" are put before us — people who are famous for being famous.

C. The fame of most entertainers, therefore,

is man-made. It is a kind of illusory magic trick. If you give thoughtless, unreflective honor to these people — imitating them and buying their products — you are being used.

D. If you ask young people why they like certain "groups" or other (temporarily) well-known entertainers, you will usually hear terms like "cool," "awesome," "great." Notice that these are not really reasons. They're vague expressions of sentiment — an emotion wrapped in a bubble of sound. People who think as vaguely as this are a huckster's dream come true.

E. Really great people are still around you. They are great for their character and their quietly heroic self-sacrifice. Open your eyes and study real people, not "celebrities." These people are worthy of your honor, and they are deeply admired by everyone who knows them well. Pray that someday you become such a person, and perhaps marry such a person.

14. "There's no such thing as a free lunch."

A. Unless you inherit great wealth, you will soon have to earn the benefits of comfort and security that you've enjoyed up to now at other people's expense. This will mean serious work.

B. You have to prepare for this eventuality by building your powers of intellect and self-control. This takes years of practice, but it results in professional success and the respect of others. Nobody respects an immature, vacillating weakling.

C. For people of competence and confidence, the world of work is mostly enjoyable. Your accomplishments bring the same happiness that amusements brought when you were a child. If you look for amusements to be your delight as a grown-up, you'll remain immature and ineffectual. You'll also be disappointed.

D. People will come to respect you for your professionalism. This professionalism means several things:
- respect for experience
- a consciousness of the need for steady self-improvement
- working to a high set of standards, whether you feel like it or not
- a sense of responsibility for the welfare of your clients and employers

You can live this professionalism, and earn people's respect for it, from the first day of your first job. Any boss can tell you that an attitude of professionalism is more important than either "talents" or educational background.

E. Professional success means several things:
- being able to support your family financially (and also with availability of time)
- doing what you sense that God has called you to do
- the joy of seeing your powers being exercised along lines of excellence.

15. "Television isn't life."

A. Television is a form of make-believe. It is not a truthful — much less authoritative — depiction of the way people live or ought to live.

B. Television personalities have an artificial-ly contrived aura of power, glamour, and limitless joy. Their off-camera lives are often deplorable and even tragic. (If they're really so happy, then why all the escapism in their lives? Why so many drug and alcohol problems? Why so much divorce and suicide?)

C. Not everyone who appears on TV is a phony. Sometimes they are people of real accomplishment in the real world. If you investigated, you'd find that such people

almost never watch television themselves; this is why they are people of
accomplishment. People who watch a lot
of TV almost never appear on it.

D. Television dramas have only an illusion of
life. Notice how seldom you ever see anyone on television in the act of working,
reading, or praying. In real life, most people do not solve problems with violence,
and most people are not obsessively preoccupied with sex.

E. Many of the people responsible for television's fare do not share our family's principles. We would be uneasy having them
as guests in our house. Why should we
cooperate with them at all?

F. A lot of sales talk on television is pitched
to our appetites and vanity. (Don't forget:
Television is not an entertainment medium really; it is a commercial medium,
whose principal purpose is to sell.) The
promises of happiness on TV are phony.
You will have to buy things all your life,
of course; but not as a passively credu-
lous "consumer."

G. For hard-working adults, television-watching functions as a pleasant relaxant. But you, as a youngster, have no need of this; you have nothing to relax from. What you need, especially at this time of life, is stimulation for your growing powers of discernment. This means books, newspapers, games, conversation. This means personal experience with real people, real situations, real problems, real ideas and ideals. You won't find these on television.

16. "School isn't life."

A. School is supposed to prepare you for the responsibilities of adult life, to build habitual powers of will and intellect through practice.

B. Adult life consists of responsible and mostly enjoyable accomplishment. The tightly structured and micro-managed environment of high school is rare in adult life. So, don't get too accustomed to it. In most of the important situations you will face later — in family and professional life — you will have to set the structures for yourself and you will have to manage your affairs.

C. Anyone old enough to go to high school is old enough to work an 8-hour day.

Throughout history and in most non-Western countries today, people of high-school age have worked at least eight hours a day, and not just for "spending money." In other words, high school in our society is an artificial prolongation of the childhood learning period. It is an expensive privilege organized and paid for by adults for your benefit. It is not a state of nature. It shouldn't be — but often is — a more high-powered form of grammar school. Adolescence is, and ought to be, a time to get serious about what you do with your mind and with your time.

D. The purpose of education is to enable you to set aside the fuzzy sentimentality of childish thinking and to make important distinctions: truth from falsehood, fact from opinion, reason from emotion, good from evil, the beautiful from the trashy. An educated person should be able to recognize bunk when he or she sees it.

E. During the years of high school, it will be largely up to you to make effective use of the abundant leisure time available to you. Read books recommended by people whose judgment you respect. Follow current events that will shape the world of your own later life. Get a part-time job and study people at work: watch who does the best work, and see if you can figure out why. Volunteer your services to people who need your help and your youthful energies.

F. In short, you will have to make an effort to overcome the normal high-school environment of irresponsible play. Start to use your increasingly powerful judgment in order to firm up your discernment of people, events, ethics, principles. High school should be a preparation for life, not one last fling at it.

G. Someone once said, "An education is what you have left over after you've forgotten the material." Sooner or later, you will forget the many facts and data that you were compelled to learn. What should remain behind is the personal strengths of mind and will that you exercised in learning them: a power of clear discernment, an ability to express your ideas clearly and convincingly, a deep understanding of people and events, a confident persistence in solving problems, a retentive memory, a respect for learning and for intellectual accomplishment, a gratitude toward the dedicated people who taught you these things — often at great personal sacrifice.

17. "Happiness comes from a strong character and a simplicity of life."

A. A strong character leads to confidence. Character is the sum total of the virtues integrated into one personality: faith, hope, charity, sound judgment (including conscience), a sense of responsibility, personal toughness, and self-control. These are strengthened and made habitual through repeated exercise.

B. The whole purpose of your upbringing is your growth in strengths of character and an internalized, habitual set of standards.

C. Aristotle said that happiness comes from the "full use of one's powers along lines of excellence."

97

D. A pile of unnecessary possessions can weigh us down, distort our priorities, and suffocate our powers of will and intellect. This is why poorer families generally turn out stronger children. People who "travel light" through life enjoy a greater spirit of adventure. A strong faith, strong will, sense of humor, ingenuity, self-respect and self-confidence — these are worth more than closets full of clothes and gadgets. Character is what you have left over if you ever go broke. People who need little are always relatively rich.

18. "Happiness comes from self-sacrificing love."

A. Love is the "life force" of everything great. Love gives meaning and greatness to all the details of everyday life. In a real sense, love is life.

B. People whose lives are moved by love never really grow old. On the other hand, younger people wholly preoccupied with themselves become precociously middle-aged.

C. Love isn't sweet sentiments. It is the willingness and ability to undergo hardship for the welfare and happiness of others.

D. The happiest people you will meet are those who devote their powers generously to the service of others.

E. When you are searching seriously for a spouse, watch closely how he or she treats the other members of his or her family. It is a preview of things to come. A young woman who is disrespectful and indifferent to parents and siblings will probably treat her husband the same way. A young man who is sneaky and distant with his present family will almost certainly treat his wife and children in the same fashion.

F. Happiness in marriage comes from a deep religious faith, lived with a spirit of loving gratitude.

G. To cut oneself off from friendship with God, either deliberately or through neglect, can lead to our earthly and eternal misery.

H. The love for God is the basis for all other great loves in life. It is the surest foundation for a family life that is profoundly happy, even in the midst of serious problems. Love leads to hope, and the Christian symbol of hope is the anchor — the tie that binds us safely to God in the middle of the storms of life.

I. As someone once said: If we really believe
    that we are guided by an all-powerful
    and all-loving God, life is a comedy.

4

STRATEGY ISSUES FOR DISCUSSION

IN THIS SECTION, like the previous one, we have assembled a series of issues for couples to think about and discuss. Each of them, we believe, is important for parents to consider deeply in order to form some strategies for the way they direct family life together.

Each of these Strategy Issues contains some statements about the dynamics of family life — sometimes direct or paraphrased comments — all drawn from the experience of "veteran" parents and insightful teachers. Together with these remarks, we have posed questions to help you direct your analysis. These are by no means exhaustive, and you could probably devise scores of others.

In some cases, of course, you may find that you do not altogether agree with the statements or with the direction of the questions.

That is not a problem. Most of these issues have much latitude of opinion and interpretation. If you do disagree, however, we would ask you to do two things. First, reflect on your reasons for disagreement, for this will throw light on your assumptions and perhaps your personal family history — matters that need clear understanding in order to form effective strategy. Secondly, we ask that you keep an open mind. Nearly all of these statements, as we've said, come from people with a great deal of experience, including great success in raising their children to responsible adulthood. All things considered, these people may be right. Decide for yourself.

As in the previous section, we would urge you to get together with other couples to discuss these issues in detail. For young couples with small children, getting together like this may pose some initial logistical problems. But other parents who have done this testify, enthusiastically, that the efforts are well worth it. Exchanging your thoughts, reactions, insights, personal experiences, stories from your own family life — all of these evoke many practical suggestions and, maybe more importantly, build your optimism and confidence.

An extra bonus to these group discussions,

perhaps the best of all, is that you and the other participants become warm, close friends. A solidarity of outlook, a shared commitment to all your children's long-term welfare, a growing respect for each other's character and convictions — what better basis is there for great friendship? If teen-agers can draw strong confidence and support from their peers, why can't their parents as well?

One final item: Don't forget to include older, more experienced parents — the "veterans" — in these discussions. Their own experiences with family life can throw a lot of light on the issues outlined here. They are, after all, the real experts — which is what you will someday be yourself, maybe sooner than you think.

Strategy Issue #1
The Problem

Has our abundant, long-lasting prosperity served to turn our young people into an artificial leisure class, a sort of home-grown aristocracy? Consider this description of a scene at the Court of Versailles about a decade before the French Revolution:

"Young aristocrats stroll idly or lounge about, looking like bored children in search of amusement. They pay no taxes and assume no real social responsibilities; their only usefulness to society is to spend unearned income. They are out of touch with the pressing social, political, and economic problems of the day. They have immediate access to food, drink, musical entertainment, games and amusements whenever they wish. They also have scarcely impeded access to drugs and promiscuous sex. Both sexes wear eye-catching hairstyles and colorful clothing, bedecked with expensive jewelry. Some, as an ironic lark, sport the clothing of the working classes, also decorated with gold and silver trinkets. Their idle conversation, punctuated by childish laughter, centers around past or upcoming dances, concerts and parties. They also gossip about each others' fashions, antics, and sexual pairings-off. From hearing their chatter, one would guess that their only real fears consist of social ostracism, growing old, sexually transmitted disease, and boredom."

This picture of life among the tiny elite of the wealthiest classes could also describe the lunch-hour scene at most large, suburban high schools — or Saturday afternoon at most suburban American shopping malls, or a warm spring afternoon at college campuses.

Q: Granted that this picture does not apply to all young people. Nevertheless, is the comparison reasonably accurate?

Q: Some have said that today's youth has inherited luxuries and perquisites that used to belong only to the very rich — and, with all this, the same vices that used to characterize the corrupt upper classes: irreligion, alcohol and drug abuse, irresponsible pleasure-pursuit, insulation from reality, and materialism. Does this generalization seem fair and reasonable?

Q: Unlike previous aristocracies, however, most of our youth will not inherit this wealth and live this way indefinitely; they must begin working in their 20's, and thus face a sudden downward social mobility. Does this reality seem related to the high suicide and depression rate among upper middle-class Western youth between the ages of 19 and 25? How does it relate to the consumerism and postponed marriages among this age group?

Strategy Issue #2
Character Formation

One experienced teacher has said the following:

"Far too many parents today seem to think that raising children right is essentially an engineering problem. They think the problem is like that of putting together the components of a stereo-system according to a set of of instructions — and they're worried because they don't have the instructions! The child didn't come with any! So they look around for the correct way to 'put the child together' so he will 'work'.... This is frustrating, because in fact there is no one, set, absolutely infallible way of dealing with kids. Children vary enormously, and what 'works' with one child can lead to rebellion in another. ... As I see it, the problem of child raising is more like farming than engineering. That is, there are several ways of raising any crop, depending on circumstances, and some tried-and-true methods generally work reasonably well. These methods you can get from other, experienced farmers; and sound approaches to dealing with different kids you can get from friendship with experienced parents — as parents have done since Adam and Eve's children came of age. Like farming, though, raising kids does seem to depend a lot on timing. There are several ways of disciplining kids, but you must do something when they're young or you'll pay for it later. Just as a farmer must plant crops in the spring, even amateurishly and imperfectly, or he won't have crops in the fall. In other words, the one serious and irremediable defect is neglect; the rest of the business is common-sense, getting reasonable-sounding advice, and trial and error.... Also, farmers know that they can only do so much with their crops and the rest is, mysteriously, in God's hands. So, too, with raising kids. Parents can only try their best and leave the rest up to God. As long as they're trying their best, even with errors along the way, they can remain at peace. God won't leave their efforts unrewarded."

Q: Is it true that neglect and inaction are the only really irremediable errors in child-raising? This would seem to imply that, as long as the parents have some strategy toward raising their children to responsible adulthood, and consciously take action to make this happen, then mistakes are relatively less important — and in any event correctible with experience and advice. Does this make sense?

Q: Teachers can verify that successful parents have many different temperaments, approaches, "house rules," and methods of discipline — and yet each of them, in different ways, have raised their children well. How does this observation square with the remarks above?

Q: Some experienced parents say that healthy self-confidence, trust in God's help, and evident unity between the spouses can compensate for any number of tactical mistakes. Does this seem reasonable? Why?

Strategy Issue #3
Raising Adults, Not Children

Nearly all successful parents, it seems, think of their children as adults-in-the-making. That is, they see themselves as raising adults, not children.

To look at it another way, they see discipline as leadership toward the acquisition of internal powers (virtues): sound judgment, a sense of responsibility, toughness ("guts," perseverance), and self-control. Discipline is a positive framework for building something, not a negative control apparatus for getting peace and quiet. Therefore, handling short-term disciplinary infractions fits into an overall strategy for building the children's lifelong character-strengths. Naturally, it is not seen this way consciously in every instance, and all parents occasionally "lower the boom" for the sake of domestic order. Nevertheless, there is a long-term strategy at work, even if it is not always consciously reflected upon.

Consciously or intuitively, such parents are working to prepare their children for a later marriage that is stable, permanent, and happy. These parents think more of their children's future life as husbands and wives, fathers and mothers — with career considerations far less important than personal character. They think of what their children will *be,* not what they will *do.*

Q: The divorce rate among younger couples is about 50%, with recent marriages lasting an average of about seven years. Given these well-publicized facts, why do so many parents fail to think much about their children's future marriage, and what needs to be done now to prepare the children well for it? Why do concerns about possible future drug-dependency far outnumber, in most parents' minds, worries about possible later marital break-up, a much more likely threat to most youngsters today?

Q: In what way(s) does a solid formation in each of the virtues — faith, hope, charity, sound judgment, sense of responsibility, toughness, self-control — contribute later to establishing a permanent, happy marriage?

Q: It is said: "Parents who work on their marriage, putting the *spouse first* and the *children second,* teach the virtues very effectively, and mainly by *example*. One hour devoted to making one's spouse happy is worth a hundred hours of lecturing the children." Does this seem correct? Was this approach, or something like it, the normal way of bringing up children before our own era?

Q: How does excessive television-watching by the children serve to weaken the effect of this example-giving?

Q: "If you prepare the kids to be successful parents, you are also preparing them for professional success, no matter what they do later for a living." Is this true?

Strategy Issue #4
Parental Example

It has been said that children's attitudes toward each parent directly reflect the parents' attitudes toward each other. That is, a husband's respect and affection toward his wife generally results in the children's respect and obedience toward her. And a wife's obvious regard for her husband's character and moral leadership results in the children's holding him in high esteem.

Consider the following testimony from a man in Colorado:

"My father died when I was an infant and my mother raised our family as a hard-working widow. All my life at home, even during adolescence, my mother could discipline me and bring me to my senses by simply saying,

'Your father would not have approved of what
you're doing right now.' ... This admonition
never failed to correct me."

Q: Does this generalization seem true —
that children mirror their parents' regard for
each other?

Q: In the case of the man quoted above,
what was the dynamic by which this
deceased father continued to influence his
children? And implicitly, what did the children learn about the character of their
mother?

Q. If this dynamic is true of most families,
what does it imply about the children's seeing (a) their father's *apparent* indifference
toward their mother, or (b) the mother's
apparent dominance over her husband in
decision-making and disciplinary matters?

Q: Since children normally do not see their
father work, they almost never witness anyone show him respect — unless this comes
from their mother. Conversely, children seldom see people show respect toward their
mother — unless it comes from their father.
What, then, follows if the children do not see

overt signs of the parents' honor and respect for each other?

Q: Since many signs of affection and respect are brief and subtle in family life, what happens if the children's attention is diverted by two or three hours of TV-watching a day?

Strategy Issue #5

The Father as Hero

Many men have a temperament (*i.e.,* a personal characteristic that cannot be easily changed) such that they have difficulty being playful and openly affectionate with somewhat older children. That is, they can be — and usually are — close and comfortable with children up to the age of two or three, but then seem to draw back considerably as the kids grow through grammar-school age. These men are comfortable with adults but not older children. They love their children deeply, but they are not easily demonstrative about it.

This sometimes causes unnecessary friction at home. The wife wonders why her husband seems detached, or less affectionate than he used to be, to the children. The husband, on his part, is annoyed with accusations that he does not deeply love the children; he *knows* this is untrue. (Generally speaking, so do the children.) Nearly all men have an instinct to play with their infant children; but, with many, this playfulness drops off as the children grow toward kindergarten age.

Interestingly, most such men find that they get along very well with their children — more than ever before, in fact — as the children grow through adolescence and become near-adults. Since men of this temperament are more comfortable with adults than children, they enjoy dealing with their nearly grown offspring, and they are often highly effective at it. If they take the trouble to step in and seriously give adult-level guidance to their adolescent kids (talking adult-to-adult, an attitude that most adolescents like), they do an excellent job in giving final finish to their children's upbringing. Their leadership at this critical juncture in the kids' lives, in fact, turns out to be at least as important as the "playfulness" that was missing earlier.

Q: If a man's temperament is like this, then why is his wife's attitude toward him —

her understanding of his deep love, despite the lack of sentimental externals — important to the children's love and respect for him? (See page 115 for the anecdote about the widow's honor for her deceased husband.)

Q: To look at it another way, how does such a man teach his children effectively by *example* rather than affectionate play? If the man cannot come down easily to the children's level, what can the wife do to bring the children up to his level — to point out to the kids that their father is a great man? (That is, that his worth is more important than his "play"?) Why is this critically important, especially later when the children are adolescents?

Q: And what can a man like this do to bring the children into the adult world where *he* is comfortable — taking them to his office, talking about his work, involving them in work around the house? All things considered, how does this approach compare with "child's-play" in shaping the children's character, and their respect for Dad?

Strategy Issue #6
Discipline as Leadership

Consider the following statements:

"Discipline doesn't just mean punishment or negative correction. Parents who see it only this way tend to become frustrated and rather paralyzed by frequent self-doubt. ... Discipline is related to the word 'disciple' — a devoted follower — and it works best when seen as positive, confident leadership toward adulthood. In a sense, conscientious parents are always 'disciplining' their children when they try to make the kids grow more confident, more responsible, more considerate, more courageous. This is done as much through affectionate teaching and encouragement as it is through correction and punishment."

"Effective parents almost always see 'no' as a loving word too. They realize that the kids' long-term best interest is more important than accommodating their misguided present whims and feelings. The affectionate imposition of 'strength-building denial' leads to the kids' present annoyance (and sometimes tears) but their future devotion to their parents.... This affectionate denial is often hard for young parents to exercise at first, but it is necessary for the youngsters' future happiness — and this urgent need is what makes conscientious parents persevere."

"One common problem for young parents is that they let their doubts lead to inaction in correcting the children. When confronted with an ambiguous corrective situation — where they're not sure what is the right thing to do — they back down, compromising their parental right (and duty) to take decisive action. The seem to confuse the rightness of a decision with their right to make a decision in the first place.... Effective and experienced parents, on the other hand, have no doubt about this right. Whether a 'judgment call' is right or wrong in a given instance is unimportant in the long run; what matters is that the children receive clear, confident moral direction from their parents, even if it's occasionally flawed with imperfect judgments. Years from now, the kids will not remember their parents' minor mistakes, but they will remember their moral leadership — and this is what counts."

Q: It is said that when parents consciously try to give good example to the children — in the way they treat each other, the way they treat God, and the way they deal with people outside the family — they are, in fact, always "disciplining" the children. Their teaching and correction thus become an *explanation* of what the kids can see for themselves. Is this true?

Q: How can parents help young children to understand that the parents' corrections and punishments derive from love? That is, the parents "hate the sin but love the sinner."

Q: Is it true that both extremes of dealing with children — permissiveness and tyranny — derive from parental self-centeredness? How so? And how do these differ from the "affectionate assertiveness" that characterizes successful parents?

Q: In most successful families, it seems, the father takes a more conspicuous and assertive role in disciplining (leading) the children as they approach and pass through adolescence. The children respond better to their father's direction at this age. Why does this happen?

Q: Many fathers effectively support their wives and discipline their teen-age children by making the following position clear: "Your mother's happiness means everything to me because she is my wife. Whatever makes her unhappy — such as your lack of cooperation — *obligates* me, as her husband, to take strong corrective action. Nobody treats my wife with disrespect,... *nobody*." Why is this stance so effective with adolescents? To what extent do they see it as fair, and therefore unarguable? What does it teach them about a husband's role toward his wife, an important concept for children nearing adulthood? How, with modification, could it also be used with younger children?

Q: Some parents say the following: "You'd go crazy trying to correct every single thing the kids do wrong. Some matters *must* be corrected every time, without fail; others, however, are 'judgment calls,' with plenty of room for leeway.... There are three areas that

require immediate and serious correction—
(a) flat defiance of authority, (b) insults or
gestures of disrespect, and (c) deliberate,
cold-blooded lying. Since the kids' future happiness depends on their honor and their
respect for parental authority, these infractions absolutely cannot be tolerated." Do you
agree with this assessment? What would be
some examples of each three categories
above? What would be examples of less-seri-
ous "judgment calls" — and what should be
done about matters that verge on the three
intolerable areas?

Q: All children, under certain circumstances, will unthinkingly and spontaneously
lie. Lying is one of their only defenses against
parental power. (The other is to weep.) But a
coldly deliberate lie is much more serious
and calls for serious punishment. Some parents, when confronted by a spontaneous lie,
tell the children to take a few minutes, think
things over, and then tell the truth *on their
honor*. This seems to teach the children that
there's a difference between "telling a lie"
and "being a liar." It also teaches much about
trust, integrity, and courageous acceptance of
just punishment (very important for the
virtues of fortitude and self-control). How can

parents, on a practical basis, distinguish between these types of lying? What should be the response (some punishment, but tempered by praise for honesty) to children who admit to having lied? What is the appropriate punishment for Lying again, even when put on one's honor?

Q: Some say, "To flatly rule out the use of force is as ineffective in child-raising as it is in international diplomacy. To young children, words alone are sometimes meaningless." To what extent, or in what circumstances, can corporal punishment be resorted to? Is it true that extensive spanking is no more effective, or even necessary, than a single, well-aimed whack? If a parent is angry, should he or she refrain from corporal punishment until later, when he/she has cooled down — or does a policy of administering only a single whack make this wait unnecessary?

Q: Is is sometimes said, "All children occasionally need a pat on the back — sometimes high, and sometimes low. It's important for kids to receive *specific praise* as well as *specific blame*. We tend to make blame specific but praise very general and vague. Kids respond well to concreteness in both areas."

Is it true that we tend to make blame much more specific than praise? What would be examples? How can praise be made more specific in family life? Is it true, also, that praise, like blame and punishment, should best be administered privately — away from the rest of the family's eyes? When should praise be public — when the whole family has been honored, when the thing praised will not incite envy?

Strategy Issue #7

Brothers and Sisters for Life

One happily married woman said the following in the course of a parenting discussion group:

"The best advice I ever received was given to me by my father when I was going off to college. He said, 'As you are approaching the age of marriage, and perhaps considering a certain young man as a future husband, do the following: take a very close look at the way he treats his brothers and sisters. Is he considerate, loyal and generous with them? Or is he indifferent, spiteful, or envious? His treatment of his siblings is a preview of the way he will treat his wife. People normally don't change overnight'."

Q: Is this advice fundamentally sound? Do adults, by and large, tend to treat their spouse and their grown siblings in a similar way?

Q: If so, could it then be said that working hard to promote loving unity among one's children (usually a very challenging job when they're young) serves to prepare them well for their future marriage? How so?

Q: Given that nearly all young children squabble and argue with siblings, at least occasionally, and given that all young married couples occasionally argue, then why is it important for parents to work hard at promoting reconciliation among the kids? What long-term benefits accrue to the children from amicable peacemaking after an argument — learning that occasional squabbles are still compatible with deep family love? How may young marriages be damaged if either spouse — or worse, both of them — failed to learn this lesson in childhood?

Q: Some parents have an iron-clad rule in family life: absolutely no harsh words or heated arguments at the dinner table. The kids can squabble elsewhere but not when the family gathers for dinner, period. Prayer before dinner sets the tone for the family meal. These parents say that the rule is sometimes tough to enforce at first but the results are worth the sacrifice. What do the children learn from this custom? What will they remember years from now about family life?

Q: Some say that *well-formed* young people generally grow closer and more affectionate with their siblings during adolescence and later, even when they frequently squabbled as young children. Does this square with your experience?

Q: Consider this statement: "The love between parents and children is the strongest bond in society. The second strongest is that between brothers and sisters. This bond, if well formed in childhood, lasts a lifetime. Being able to count on the love and support of one's siblings is one of the greatest sources of strength in life." Is this true?

Strategy Issue #8
Adolescence

Some observers have noted that there are three periods in life when hormonal interactions in the body produce psychological reactions, a kind of mild temporary insanity: mood-swings, crankiness, lack of self-esteem, resistance to correction, unreasonable worries, stubbornness, escapism, and other unpleasantries. The first of these occurs between the ages of two and four. The second, just as dramatic but varying considerably from person to person, takes place in adolescence, from 13 to 17 or later. The third, much more subtle and subdued, occurs around the age of 40, plus or minus a few years. This last stage is not universal and varies a great deal, but it is quite common.

Q: Some experienced parents have said that the best way for parents to handle their children's adolescence is with (a) the same steadiness of guidance exercised when they were small youngsters, (b) a lot of patience, confident that they will eventually snap out of it, (c) affectionate understanding combined with firmness of leadership in matters of moral principle, and (d) a sense of humor. Do these observations seem reasonable?

Q: These parents, all of whom raised several children, have said that, as each of the kids successively passed through both trying periods, their own parental attitudes gradually changed. Over time, they as parents shifted from fearful apprehension (often exasperation) to cautious optimism and finally to confident detachment (with even some amusement). This happened as each of the children went through the 2-to-4 period and then later through adolescence. Why did this change of attitudes by the parents take place?

Q: Much has been written in recent years about the so-called "mid-life crisis," which seems to describe the third subtle period mentioned above. Like the first two, it is temporary but mildly-to-seriously troublesome. In many families, unfortunately, both the parents (or one of them) and the adolescents may be simultaneously out of kilter — with an excessive touchiness and ill-humor on both sides. What can parents do to ride this period through? (And, interestingly, could the temporary nature of this parental third period be related to the attitude-shift described in the previous question?)

Q: Is there any truth to the following statement? — Most children who retain strong respect for their parents have relatively few serious problems in adolescence. Much of the "bad press" about adolescence has come from permissively minded "parenting" authors, who have generalized about their own bad experience with their spoiled children in the teen years, along with that of their like-minded associates and friends. Their problems have not been, by any means, universal. In other words, publicity about adolescence has been skewed by what statisticians call a "sampling bias." Does this seem reasonable?

Strategy Issue #9
Television as Rival

Given the importance of example in forming the mind and will of children, what influence does extensive and indiscriminate television watching have on youngsters? Consider the following:

What do the children *not* witness on television? They do *not* see people work, pray, read books, discuss ideas and events, or engage in any activity that is dramatically "boring." Ironically, television-watching is so boring in itself that we very seldom see anyone on television actually watching television. They also almost never see elderly people or clergy portrayed realistically, as anything other than caricatures. They do not see people exercise discriminating judgment, shrewd assessment of people, a sense of responsibility, perseverant problem-solving, or self-control. It's arguable that TV attractively portrays the exact *opposite* of these virtues. They do not see any professions portrayed except law-enforcement (a preposterous caricature, at that) and entertainment.

While engaged in TV-watching, what do the children fail to see, hear, and do at home? What gets displaced? The children do not talk much with other members of the family. They do not learn much, therefore, about what goes on in the mind of their parents, especially their father: opinions, convictions, life at work outside the family, reactions to current events, personal history of the parents, the lives and accomplishments of grandparents, people whom the parents admire (and why), assessments of people and local affairs, and so on — the whole range of the parents' thoughts. judgments, and values. They also miss out in games, reading, and conversation with siblings — with whom they share family life for only 15 to 18 years or less before separating permanently. They also fail to *overhear* conversation between parents, or between parents and adult guests — a subtle way by which children have always learned much about adult-level thinking and friendship.

Q: Given that children's minds are specially equipped to learn through trial-and-error activity (the whole purpose, it seems, for their innate curiosity), then what effect can prolonged, passive inactivity have upon them? Is a natural learning process going unexercised?

Q. If children learn about life from what they witness, what can happen if TV presents them (from their perspective) with people apparently taking turns to (a) entertain and amuse them, and (b) sell products through appeals to vanity, appetites, and desire for conformity? How is this phenomenon related to children's very common complaint that something is "boring"?

Q: Is it true, as many maintain, that boredom comes principally from having a power (mental or physical) that is going unexercised — an ability that is not being put to productive, and therefore enjoyable, use? (Under what circumstances, for instance, would a gifted writer be bored? A skilled athlete? A talented engineer?) What powers or talents are children strengthening, if any, while watching hours of TV? Could this vacuum be related to complaints of boredom?

Q: Clearly, not all television-watching is a waste of time. Much of what appears on TV is useful, even beneficial, to family life. Many parents have the following criteria for selecting television programs: (a) whatever serves to bring the family together in a group-spectator way, actually promoting conversation during and after the event (sports, Presidential addresses, special performances by outstanding artists, well-done entertainment, etc.); (b) whatever promotes fuller understanding of science, history, current affairs (documentaries, interviews with experts, news programs). What else might be included under these two broad areas? What would clearly be left out?

Q: Under what circumstances can watching sports events and artistic performances actually enhance family solidarity? But under what conditions could this viewing go too far, to the point of encroaching on the family's life together?

Q: Consider this fact: If the text from a 30-minute news program were written and laid out as newsprint, it would cover only the first page of an average-sized newspaper. Why, then, should television news not form the

137

family's only source of current-affairs awareness? What accounts for the observation among teachers that most high-school and even college students are seriously deficient in understanding current public issues, or the historical circumstances behind them?

Q: Is it true that children learn much about their parents' judgment, in indirect and subtle ways, by the parents' *reactions* to television — what programs they select or ignore, which they prohibit or turn off in mid-broadcast, which comments or arguments they utter in reaction to what's being said on TV (arguing with the television, as it were), and so forth? Can it be said that the parents' evident discernment and rational control in using TV are more beneficial to the children's judgment-formation than a blanket prohibition of all TV use in the home?

Strategy Issue #10
Media "Heroes"

Consider these three generalizations:

"Every culture in history has presented young people with heroes to pattern their lives after — men and women who personified strengths of character and who accomplished great deeds in the fulfillment of responsibilities. These came in religious lore, national history, and literature."

"If kids do not have heroes to emulate, then they follow after clowns."

"Kids' attraction to entertainers and rock-culture figures seems proportional to their lack of real respect for their parents. If the parents seem weak (deficient in powers of judgment, responsibility, toughness, and self-

control), then the children pull toward char-
acters who seem comparatively more powerful and interesting. On the other hand, those
youngsters who deeply respect their parents'
strengths can take or leave rock/entertain-
ment figures. Their interest is mild to begin
with, and it is based mostly on conformity to
the teen culture, not genuine personal admiration; eventually the kids outgrow it. In
other words, a high regard for one's parents
usually thwarts or minimizes peer pressures
toward the rock-drug-sex culture."

Q: Who were the most common heroes presented to youth of our country — from literature, religion, national history — up to about
a generation ago? In what way(s) did each
personify the virtues: faith, hope, charity,
sound judgment and conscience, responsibility, toughness, self-control? (Insightful exercise: Ask your children what they know about
each of these figures whom you and your parents were led to admire. Be prepared for a
surprise.)

Q: At what age should children learn that
the *persona* of entertainers is mostly make-
believe and commercialized hokum? A great
many of these people, despite outward
appearances of happy success, are often

deeply troubled and messed up in their personal lives — as evidenced by their escapism, drug and alcohol problems, and even suicides. How can kids be brought to see this effectively?

Q: Why do so many parents hesitate to prohibit morally offensive music-lyrics inside their homes? What is the best way to draw the line between acceptable and unacceptable teen-culture accoutrements: music, publications, videos, posters, dress and the like?

Q: Some parents have a rule: "This home is owned and run by us, the parents, and *we* decide what is or is not welcome under our roof. Whatever offends our moral principles, whatever tends to undo our teachings of right and wrong, and whatever portrays human beings as mere objects — these things will not enter our home, either physically or electronically, no matter who pays for them." This stance cannot shield the children from exposure to offensive materials (realistically, of course, nothing can do this), but it does strongly teach the parents' principles and their exercise of responsible moral judgment—which is what the children need to take through life. Does it seem workable as an operating principle? Would it seem fair or unfair to the children? (Young people generally accept, albeit reluctantly at first, a rule that seems tough but eminently fair.)

Q: Is the following statement true? — "When parents exercise control over the media, when they say who or what is permitted in the home, they then appear to the children as stronger, more powerful than the various 'celebrities.' In the rivalry for the children's admiration, they win." In light of the rock-culture's allurements to young adolescents, why is this "victory" important?

Strategy Issue #11
Real Heroes

One of the effects of modern life has been that parents are generally isolated from other adults. Relatives live at some distance and neighbors are only light acquaintances. One of the results of this is that children scarcely know any adults outside the family. They do not know whom their parents admire, and they almost never see other adults show respect through friendship with their parents. And, of course, if the kids' attention is overly distracted through excessive TV-watching, then the children hardly know their parents either; thus they hardly know *any* adults apart from those shown on the tube.

Q: Is it true that all real friendship is ultimately based on respect, which in turn derives from perception of character strengths — the greater the mutual respect, the more cordial the friendship? If children see few friends in their parents' lives, therefore, what are they *not* learning about character? Is it true, in other words, that children learn to assess character by seeing whom their parents admire, and why? If so, what happens if the parents *appear* to admire *only* the "celebrities" on television?

Q: Given how very hard life was for our forebears earlier in this century (say, before 1945), can it truly be said that *all* of us are descended from heroic people? What can be done to teach the children about the quietly heroic sacrifices of their grandparents, great-grandparents, and earlier forebears, including their loyalty to our family's religious faith? What could the children learn thereby about family honor, family "name," and faithfulness to religious heritage?

Q: Some say that boys are strongly attracted to dedicated coaches because these men are the only adult males whom the boys see up close actually *working* — exercising judgment, responsibility, courageous perseverance, and self-control under challenging circumstances. Coaches today seem to fill the role that fathers formerly did inside the family, giving daily example of how character-strengths are exercised in adult life. What can fathers do today to help their children learn about their own lives as responsible breadwinners? How does extensive conversation fit into this? And how is TV an obstacle to this knowledge?

Q: All parents seem to need advice and support from close friends. Parents today have to work at this to make it happen. How do parenting discussion groups help to meet this real, perfectly normal human need? Is it true that parents generally need *encouragement* every bit as much as detailed practical *advice* — that is, an ongoing affirmation that their judgment is fundamentally sound and they are on the right track?

Strategy Issue #12

Education & Upbringing

There have been two fundamentally different philosophies regarding the upbringing of children, including their education in school.

The traditional one holds that children are born with a fallen nature, and they therefore have to be taught right conscience and strengths of character — through word, example, and directed practice — as they grow up. Otherwise they arrive at adulthood with the ego and appetites of childhood. The role of school, therefore, is to strengthen the faculties of intellect, imagination, and will, as well as impart adult-level standards of responsible performance.

The other, more recent viewpoint maintains that children are born intrinsically good but are corrupted by the forces of adult society, against which they must be protected. The good qualities of childhood — spontaneity, frankness, curiosity, etc. — must be cultivated. This happens through exercise of self-expression, giving free rein to one's "feelings," and promoting "sincerity" for its own sake. Rules, restrictions, limits and the like are seen as encroachments or inhibitions upon a child's natural good qualities and self-esteem.

In other words, the traditional view sees upbringing as a process of building strengths; the alternative view sees it as preserving innate goodness. One seeks to prepare the children for the realities of adult life; the other looks to maintain the qualities of childhood. One seeks to build self-confidence through exercise of directed, responsible accomplishment; the alternative wants young people to "feel good about themselves" through frank self-expression and other artistic activities. Broadly speaking, the older view sought to foster children's relations with *external* reality, the world as adults know it. The more recent view cultivates children's interactions with *inner* reality, the inner "self" and feelings. (These generalizations are simplified but, we believe, not overly so.)

147

Q: No one can hold a theory or principled position unless there is *some* truth to it; if it were entirely false, no reasonable person would believe in it. What real truths about life and childhood lie at the center of both these positions? What is being exaggerated or oversimplified?

Q: Consider this statement: "Many schools seem bent on having children retain essentially the same outlook and personal habits they had in kindergarten. Judging by what you see in a great many adolescents and college students, they are highly successful at this." Is this judgment fair? Do many schools, even high schools, over-emphasize play, games, amusements, and the television culture?

Q: It is said that the best teachers and coaches in a school system, regardless of the system's official educational philosophy, are those who still see their role as that of building inner strengths: judgment, responsibility, perseverance, and self-control. Consciously or intuitively these professionals try to prepare the children for future competence regardless of later career-choice. Is this true? Is it also true that children generally hold such teach-

148

ers and coaches in high esteem, and remember them years later? Why does this happen?

Q: It has been said, "An education is what you have left over after you've forgotten the material." What habits of mind and will should students have by age 18 — with respect to (a) discerning truth from specious falsehood, (b) confidence in approaches to problem-solving, (c) criteria for evaluating people, current affairs, political and social issues, (d) respect for intellectual and artistic accomplishment, (e) an interest in reading (literature, biography, science, history), (f) ability to express one's thoughts (not just "feelings") in an interesting and persuasive way, especially in writing?

Q: If schools are deficient in building these powers, how can parents foster them at home? What role does the parents' own example play in this?

Q: An Oxford professor once said that the purpose of an education is that "young people can recognize bosh when they see it." This would seem to imply that young people should be led to recognize the true, the good, and the beautiful — and distinguish these

149

from the evil, the false, and the ugly. How does this power of *discernment* fit with the traditional educational philosophy? Or with the modern one, much more common today? What can be done at home in the youngest years to foster the development of this power?

Q: Related to the above question, consider this: "One of the best things parents can do with television is to *argue with it*. Kids can learn a lot from their parents' critical reactions to what appears on the tube — scoffs, rebuttals, agreement, ridicule, satire, expressions of admiration or distaste, or just plain shutting the thing off. The TV does serve as a means of pointing out the false, the evil, the tasteless, and the ugly." Is this true? What can children learn from watching their parents' react to television fare? In other words, is there such a thing as active TV-watching?

Strategy Issue #13
Religious Strength

Consider the following remarks from an experienced teacher:

"Most conscientious parents today will admit that *materialism* is the greatest moral evil threatening their children. But I think they misunderstand what this term means. Most people associate it with money, cars, luxuries, and the like, and they see these things as the problem — though parents usually have trouble explaining why. But consumer goods and money are only tangentially related to the problem.... The real evil of materialism is to consider *man* as a *thing*. The belief that man is essentially a mere object — a cunning animal, as some would put it — is what we're really up against. A materialist in this sense would thus put other things (money, power, luxuries, comfort, convenience) ahead of the rights and sensibilities of other people, who are treated as mere things. This irreligious, and even inhuman. mind-set accounts for so many of the evils we see today: pornography, violence, fraud, marital break-up, abortion, drugs, and so much else. The principal cause of this corruptive life-outlook is the decline of religion, the loss of a sense of accountability before God or even life after death. As Pope John Paul II has said, the 'death of God' leads directly to the 'death of man.'"

Q: Is this true? Is the problem of materialism more a matter of attitude toward God and others rather than mere pursuit of money and luxuries? Can we possess and use material goods, even expensive ones, without falling into materialism? Do you know people who are like this, who are reasonably well-off but deeply religious and considerate?

Q: Materialism has been called the great evil of the 20th century, applying to the "consumerism" of the West and the "collectivism" of this century's great "gangster-states." Does the definition above apply to both forms? Is there a relation between evils of Western society (abortion, pornography, divorce) and those of the collectivist political systems (genocide, terrorism, concentration camps)? If the problem is essentially religious, then does the answer also lie in religion?

Q: Statistical studies show that young people from homes where both parents seriously practice their religion have a much lower incidence of problems in life. For these young adults, the rates of drug-abuse, illegitimate pregnancy, suicide, and divorce are substantially lower than "normal." Why should this be? How does this phenomenon square with the remarks above?

Q: It has been said that one of the great illusions of Western life in our time is that *everything is under control:* that is, our unprecedented, prolonged prosperity has created the impression, especially among young people, that peace and great abundance are a "state of nature" — that war and economic disaster are things of the past, phenomena that will not reoccur in our lifetime. This, in turn, leads to a diminishment of religious faith, a consciousness that we depend on God's help and mercy. Does this seem true? Is it likely, all things considered, that peace and prosperity will continue unchanged over the next 60+ years — the lifetime of today's children? If a serious international or economic crisis were to happen later (and some believe this is plausible, even likely, given historical trends), how important will strong religious faith be to today's children?

Q: For Christians, the symbol of hope (trust in God's loving Providence) has been the anchor — the tie that holds us safely through the storms of life. What can happen to children later if they must face some serious personal crisis (drugs or alcohol, marital problems, financial troubles, etc.) and do *not* have faith in God's help? Why is it critically important for children to understand what St. Paul said: "For those who love God, *all things* work together unto good"?

Q: Statistics show that by the year 2010 the number of priests in the U.S. will drop by more than half, from today's 45,000 to less than 21,000. This will mean, among other things, increased hardship and sacrifice in fulfilling even the minimal practices of faith. How so? Given the propensity of people to abandon what is difficult, or even inconvenient, what will be the likely effects of this drop-off in the way today's children will live their religion 20 or 30 years from now? What sort of commitment toward religious sacrifice, therefore, do today's children need to acquire? And what could happen to *their* children later if they neglect or abandon their religion because it's "too much trouble"?

Q: What can today's parents do to strengthen — by word, example, and practice — their children's religious faith? How do the following fit into this teaching process — regular (even daily) religious worship, dressing up for church, time set aside for family prayer, religious pictures and symbols in the home, prayer before meals, financial and other support for the church, friendship with the clergy, asking children for their prayers, visiting the sick and elderly, making an annual retreat?

Q: Over the last two generations, there has been a general drop-off in religious belief and practice. Why can it be said that today's parents — for the sake of their children and grandchildren — can and must turn this around? What could happen if they do not?

Strategy Issue #14
Will-Power and Self-Control

Consider the following remarks from experienced parents and teachers:

"Adversity strengthens character."

"I know there are exceptions to this rule, but I think it's generally true: Children who are taught considerateness and good manners at the youngest age grow up to be chaste in high school and young adulthood. They respect other people, and people respect them. Eventually, and usually unwittingly, they wind up marrying spouses who are similar to their own parents in outlook and character."

"The words *please* and *thank you* are not just social embellishments. For children they are the first, necessary steps toward living like civilized people instead of technically skilled barbarians."

"A great many parents give in to their children's wishes about fashionable dress and gadgets because they don't want the kids to suffer from being *different,* out of step with the very latest 'in' things. In doing this, they teach the children a potentially dangerous attitude: that *conformity is very important* and that 'being different' is to be avoided at all costs. Why don't they see the dangers of this outlook? ... What could happen to the kids later in high school, when alcohol or drugs are being passed around at parties? Or in college, when 'everyone else' is sexually promiscuous? Or as young singles, when most of one's acquaintances are 'living together' with someone? ... Anyone who aims to live a moral life has to become accustomed to being 'different.' A habit of mindless conformity can lead to endless personal suffering."

"Being 'poor in spirit' (a Christian virtue) means being *detached* from things — being able to 'take them or leave them,' being able to possess goods without being possessed by

157

them. It means, among other things, putting people ahead of possessions — and, in a sense, seeing material things (including money) only as instruments for serving God and the needs of others."

Q: More than one teacher has said: "In the first couple of weeks of the school year, I can generally spot children who come from larger families. They seem to have more healthy self-confidence, more initiative and reliability, more patience with setbacks, more ability to get along well with others." How does this observation fit with the remarks above?

Q. Under what circumstances should children witness their parents living gratitude and good manners toward each other? Since all courtesy is based on implicit respect, what do the children learn about the parents' attitudes toward each other when good manners are habitually practiced at home?

Q: Is the following statement true? — "Adults almost always respect youngsters who show good manners, and they grow to respect the parents for this courtesy in the children." If so, why does this happen? What does habitual courtesy among children signify about their family life?

Q: Many parents, even when they can afford to spend the money, deliberately make children wait a while before purchasing a fashionable item. They say, for instance, "We'll talk about it in six weeks." Moreover, they purposely avoid making impulse purchases, especially of expensive items. What does this deliberate waiting period teach the children? How is this lesson reinforced by having the children also earn, at least partly, what they want to buy? (And parenthetically, what is the normal life of a current fashion in dress or electronic gadgets? Weeks? Months? What does this waiting period teach about the passing nature, and even the artificiality, of fashionably "hot items"?)

Q. Is it true that children with deep respect for their parents are generally attracted to suitors who resemble them?

Q. The term "class" in people is elusive to define, though we generally recognize and respect it. How would you define it? (Try making a list of people in public life, including entertainers and screen actors, identifying those with "class" and those without.)

How is "class" related to habitual courtesy? To habitual self-restraint? To genuine considerateness?

Q. Experts have noted that young people with alcohol and drug problems nearly always have a personal history of indulgence in food and drink — candy, pastries, soft drinks, snacks. Does this stand to reason? Aside from dietary and weight-control considerations, what advantages accrue to children by limiting or delaying "junk food" intake? (Parenthetical observation: Diabetics generally have rather strong will-power.)

Q: To get a clearer picture of "needs" in the home, try this: Make a list of the gadgets and amusements that did not exist in the home in, say, 1973 — then 1963, then 1953. Since there are only so many hours in the day when a family is together (roughly a constant over the past 40 years, or even less), then what activities have these items replaced?

Q: One of the more recent moral developments is that of treating *age* as the dividing line between good and evil: "Children under 17 not admitted," "For mature audiences only," "Parental guidance suggested." What can parents do to show children that age is irrelevant to serious moral matters, that sexual immorality is unacceptable for adults as well? What should be symbolically excluded from the home?

Q: Some parents give the following explanation to children: "We will have nothing enter this home — magazines, television shows, movies, songs, posters, whatever — that offends God and treats other people as mere things. This goes for gratuitous violence as well as pornography. It also goes for entertainers and performers who promote this life-outlook by word and example.... When the children are grown and gone, they can live according to their own conscience. But *our* conscience, here and now, says we will not have it in the house." How does this criterion — "God does not want us to treat other people like objects" — help parents to draw the line for children? How does it reinforce family solidarity and considerateness?

Strategy Issue #15

Perseverance and Confidence

A number of studies over the years have tried to account for professional and business success — that is, which background factors (economic and social origins, types of education, personal traits and temperament, etc.) could be found in common among most successful men and women.

Oddly enough, these people seem to have had remarkably little in common. They varied enormously in family background circumstances, extent and quality of education, "managerial style," and even personal temperament. Two traits have stood out, however, as common to almost all of them. First, they displayed a confident self-assurance that inspired people's respect, even devotion.

Secondly, they have had an ability to concentrate their full attention to a task at hand; they could make good use of time, even odd moments, and they could work almost anywhere.

Q: It is said that children learn confidence in several ways: (a) by seeing others have confidence in them, (b) by contributing to the needs of others, (c) by pitting their powers against problems and overcoming these successfully, (d) by learning, through experience, that responsibility calls on us to surpass ourselves. How do family chores, homework, hobbies, and athletics contribute to this confidence building in children?

Q: Consider this statement from a teacher: "Parents who do too much for the kids (completing school projects for them, for instance) are doing them a long-term disservice. Children need a chance to make mistakes, to learn how they can cope with tough realities successfully." Is it true that children need to be *directed* by adults, but not *managed* by them? What is the difference?

Q: Another quote: "One big problem with American children today is that they are micro-managed by adults up to early high school and then they have almost no supervision whatever. They go from a superabundance of adult help to practically none at all." Given that this view might be exaggerated, is there any truth to it? If so, what is the preferred alternative? Should children receive, as many parents say, a steady *direction* (but not management) all the way from infancy to college and even later?

Q. Are the following generalizations true? Parents who *manage* say to the children, "Let me do this for you." In adolescence, then, the children reject or ignore the parents' help because they want to do everything for themselves. Those parents who *direct,* however, say to the children, "You can do this job yourself, and try doing it this way." These youngsters, in adolescence and later, then have a habit of turning to their parents for *advice.* In other words, those parents who *direct* form a lifelong bond of mutual trust and confidence with their children.

Q: It is said that all societies progress through a kind of social contract between the elders and youth. A team dynamic drives the society: older people provide the experience, and young people provide the energy. Together, they make things happen. In what way do confident *directive* parents (as described above) bring this dynamic to family life? And what happens in those other families when lack of communication deprives the children of parental experience, while the children's energy goes exclusively into play? How does television-watching fit into this dynamic?

Q: Consider this statement: "At some point, children need to learn that fear is beside the point. Fear of pain, disappointment, inconvenience, social ostracism — these are a constant in life and should have no influence on our doing what's right, what duty calls for. Courageous people act *despite* anxieties, not *without* them. The greater the fears they have to overcome or ignore, the more courageous they are." How important is it for children to hear from time to time, "You can do it; just give it a try"? To what extent, and in what ways, should children learn about the difficulties and worries that their parents have to contend with?

Q: One parent said this: "Isn't it remarkable how the experiences that were awful to

165

go through are later the most fun to look back on? Our family once had a disastrous vacation trip, where everything went wrong and we suffered through days of mishaps and agony. It has entered into family lore, and we've laughed about it for more than 20 years. The other trips, where everything went smoothly — we don't remember a thing about them." How important is it for children to see their parents' attitudes of detachment and a sense of humor in the face of setbacks and adversity? ("We might as well laugh at this now, because we will later!") How does religious faith contribute to this detachment and humor — and the children's overall confidence?

Strategy Issue #16
Family Life as Adventure

Consider the following remarks from a long-time observer of family life:

"It seems that middle-class parents today can be divided into two groups — those who see family life as a *picnic*, and those who see it as a *game*.

"The picnickers view family life as a kind of static, leisurely, sit-down sampling of various pleasurable delights. The family members see shared comfort and amusements as the family's first order of business, and boredom is the enemy. In far too many cases, however, the parents lose out. Sooner or later, and especially in adolescence, the children drift away to pursue other, more high-powered delights — some of them dangerous and even tragic. Picnics are only delightful for the first couple of courses; eventually, boredom brings matters to a close.

"The other parents, by and large the successful ones, see their task as a lively, purposeful, athletic pursuit. The goal, always before their eyes, is the way their children will turn out as adults. To this end, they struggle hard. They seem to experience all the agony and enjoyments of a hard-fought game — with its ups and downs, reverses and advances, bruises and delights, and a growing sense of confidence as they near their goal. All things considered, a game is much harder than a picnic — but much more richly rewarding.

"When the children are grown and gone, the adventurous parents can enjoy the fruits of their 20-year struggle: seeing their children continue the game of life themselves. For the picnickers, however, their problems are often only just beginning.

"So, to young parents, I'd say this: Set high ideals for your children and be prepared for a challenging struggle. But hang in there. Your sacrifices last for only a few years, and they're well worth the trouble. Someday your children will look back on their family life with admiration and gratitude."

Q: How do these two descriptions of family life (picnic vs. game) fit what we've seen in this book about successful parents?

Q. Regarding those parents who treat family life as a game — what are they competing against? Is it the environment, or is it the baggage of faults and weaknesses in their children?

Q. Is it true what these remarks seem to imply — that parents either make sacrifices now or pay later? In what sense, then, is dedicated character-formation really an investment?

AFTERWORD:

A FINAL NOTE TO PARENTS

It should be clear from everything in this book that raising children well is frequently difficult, often very challenging. It is do-able, as countless parents have proved, but not easily. Nothing worthwhile is ever easy. The tasks before you as parents may therefore seem daunting. Consequently, we would like to leave you here with some final thoughts for your consideration, and encouragement.

For conscientious parents with strong convictions, family life is indeed an adventure. Raising one's children to responsible adulthood is life's greatest challenge, and in fact its greatest reward.

But bear this in mind from time to time, if only to retain your peace of mind: The greatest adventures in history hardly seemed that way, at the time, to the people who lived through them. Though these people started off with high, clear ambitions and much enthusiasm, their forward progress invariably ran into setbacks, obstacles, hardship — one tough situation after another. Adventures always mean challenge, and challenge always means hard work and sacrifice. No ideal ever becomes a reality without sacrifice.

Nonetheless, they persevered and finally triumphed. As they achieved their goal, and looked back on what they had gone through, only then could they say with satisfaction: "We made it! And wasn't that a great adventure! "

Raising your children right will involve, inevitably, this same succession of setbacks and triumphs, troubles and advances, disappointments and laughter. But if you persevere courageously, trusting in God's help, you will win. Your children will look back on their lives with you and say, with gratitude and admiration, "Mom and Dad were great people."

Isn't *greatness* what you want for your children? When all is said and done, that is the ambition of all conscientious parents, that their children grow to become great men

171

and women.

Someone once said, "A great man is one who does not lose the heart that he had as a child." A wise insight. Each child should grow to have strength of mind and will, full maturity of development. But all his life, he should retain the heart that he had in childhood — a trusting love for his parents, a sincere confidence in God, a devotion to his family, an openness to friends, a direct gaze on the truth.

Any man or woman who retains this heart through life will be known as great, even if only to family and friends and God.

The heartfelt warmth of family solidarity has been symbolized throughout history by the image of the hearth. Your own home is a hearth, and so it should be.

But as you sacrifice to raise your children, remember this: sometimes our perspective is slanted askew if we approach too close to things.

Sometimes you, like so many other parents before you, may be tempted to discouragement by the mess that so often surrounds you. The piles of laundry, the tasks to be done, the bickering of the kids, the struggles with manners and cleanliness and homework, on and on seemingly without end — all these things can produce discouragement and make parents wonder, "Are we getting anywhere? Are we accomplishing anything?"

Yes, you are. At times like this, turn your mind toward the hearth. If you approach very close to a hearth-fire, only inches away, what do you see? Ashes, dirt, chaotic jumble, seemingly pointless destruction and waste.

It's only when you step back from the hearth-fire and view it from a distance that its true worth becomes clear. It shines forth as a symbol of the family — unity in diversity, a splendid thing of light and warmth and beauty.

So bear this distant vision in mind from time to time when you find yourself too close to the fire. This vision of your family life together, with all its light and warmth and beauty, is what your grown children will look back on — and the light from that fire will brighten all the pathways of their lives.

Index